J. Calvin Coolidge:

Letters from the Korean War

PRAISE FOR...

J. Calvin Coolidge: Letters from the Korean War

"*J. Calvin Coolidge: Letters from the Korean War* is a timely and excellent book by Lisa Soland that follows the life of a forgotten American hero who served his nation during the Korean War. The pinnacle of this book captures the battle of King's Hill (Hill 902) in North Korea, where Calvin and his unit faced a massive assault by the communist forces. Despite being massively outnumbered, Calvin's unit beat back the Reds, although at a great cost in lives. Calvin himself was seriously wounded in this action. I highly recommend this book that revives the memory of a great American and reminds us of the great sacrifice that comes with our freedoms."

Senator Doug Mastriano, PhD, Colonel, US Army (retired)

"It is often said that newspapers are pages of American history, written one day at a time. The same holds true for letters from soldiers facing enemies half a world away. In Lisa Soland's latest book, these up-close accounts were penned by her uncle, J. Calvin Coolidge, during the Korean War. Unlike his storied namesake, this Coolidge wasn't silent, for which readers and historians can be thankful."

Sam Venable, author and columnist, Knoxville News Sentinel

"*J. Calvin Coolidge: Letters from the Korean War* is a very interesting multi-sided book based on letters shared by members of the Coolidge family about the latest happenings where they are living. Lisa Soland, a noted author and niece of the central character, collected and transcribed the letters. J. Calvin Coolidge was a soldier who was involved (including being wounded) in the Korean War. The various letters give an insight into the lives and opinions of family members during a troubled time in our history. *J. Calvin Coolidge: Letters from the Korean War* is a must-read, especially for folks interested in this particular period."

Michael F. Dilley, Military Historian and Author

"I highly recommend *J. Calvin Coolidge: Letters from the Korean War*, compiled by Lisa Soland. Lisa is an excellent author who again has captured the imagination using personal pictures and letters of J. Calvin Coolidge. Her work is always an outstanding effort of using original documents and first account information to write an informative and interesting book. She used these skills to research through interviews with family members and original documents to write an excellent play, *Sergeant York*, about my grandfather, Sgt. Alvin C. York. She is an extremely talented writer who captures the story in a delightful, easy-to-read story. You will not be disappointed in spending time with this book."

Gerald York, COL (ret), USA, and Grandson of Sgt. Alvin C. York

"Perhaps there is no better lasting legacy for a President of the United States than to have a newborn child become his namesake. Such was the case for our 30th President of the United States, John Calvin Coolidge (1872-1933). On April 24, 1926, Franklin Pierce Coolidge and Doris Elizabeth Nesbit named their firstborn child after his famous distant cousin—8th cousins twice removed, to be exact. *J. Calvin Coolidge: Letters from the Korean War*, edited by his niece, Lisa Soland, is both a tribute to her uncle and their shared Coolidge family heritage in America that dates back to 1630. By gathering and annotating an impressive collection of personal letters, newspaper clippings, and photographs, Lisa has enabled her uncle's story to be told in his own words, with appropriate annotations as needed. Clearly, President Coolidge and his namesake cousin shared much more than a name. Both lived in Western Massachusetts; both served their country; both chronicled their lives through their letters and photographs. And both men shared a blend of wit and wisdom that is so characteristic of New Englanders. Lisa's well-researched and well-written book will serve as an inspiration for anyone thinking about compiling a family memoir of their own."

Tracy W. Messer, APR, Living History Performer as "President Calvin Coolidge," and Coolidge Ambassador for the Calvin Coolidge Presidential Foundation, Inc.

J. Calvin Coolidge

Letters, Photographs, and Artifacts from the

KOREAN WAR

J. CALVIN COOLIDGE: LETTERS FROM THE KOREAN WAR
Compiled, transcribed, and edited by Lisa Soland

Published in 2022 by:
Climbing Angel Publishing
P.O. Box 32381
Knoxville, Tennessee 37930
http://www.ClimbingAngel.com

First Edition, July 2022
Printed in the United States of America
Cover and Interior design by Climbing Angel Publishing
Special Photo Editing by Shawn Williams

ISBN: 978-1-956218-19-0
Library of Congress Control Number: 2022906401

This labor of love is dedicated to my late uncle,
J. Calvin Coolidge,
his wife Christy, and my mother and father,
Ann and Norman J. Soland

CONTENTS

INTRODUCTION

My uncle, J. Calvin Coolidge, came to live with our family in Spring Grove, Illinois, in 1972. He had been living in New Salem, Massachusetts, with his mother, Doris, since his father Franklin died on December 8, 1968. Calvin was a farmer, primarily growing fruits and vegetables like his father. I remember my uncle being larger than life and always singing or whistling a 1940s tune. The speed at which he moved matched the tempo of the song, and he was always moving.

My mother, Ann, created space for Calvin in our recreation room, where we played pool and air hockey, but it was also where my mother did the laundry. The area now housed a twin-sized bed for my uncle Cal. We never saw him in it. Like my parents, he was always up before any of us kids. My father, Norman, made our kitchen table. He designed it like a picnic table you'd find at a park. We needed the two long benches on either side to sit the 10 of us—seven kids, Mom, Dad, and Cal.

My father had offered my uncle a job to work with him in his landscaping business, and when there wasn't enough work, Cal planted our family garden. We had more than enough of everything, and on occasion, I helped. I loved working alongside Cal. I loved to hear him sing. During our time together, he would eventually get around to singing "Mona Lisa." I have always thought of that Nat King Cole tune as our song. Throughout those passing years, I never asked my uncle if he was sharing it on my account. I just decided he was, and it made me feel special. During my efforts to compile this book, I encountered some difficulties, as one does with these projects. I called out to our modern music box and asked, "Alexa, play some Nat King Cole music," and the song "Mona Lisa" rang out. I could almost hear my uncle whispering, *"Don't worry about it. Everything's going to be fine."*

While my uncle was living with us, I learned more about him, primarily that he had fought in the Korean War and had been shot. Calvin told us (his niece and nephews) that the bullet was still precariously lodged in his body. The shell lay just a fraction of an inch away from his spine. He explained that the doctors could not remove the bullet because it was too close to the spinal cord and if their hands slipped during surgery, he could become paralyzed for life. I must say, I was afraid for Cal my entire life. It wasn't until sorting through these inherited artifacts that I learned this was not the case. As he jumped into a nearby trench in the battle of King's Hill, the bullet that hit my uncle entered his body and *exited* his body. (See the letter dated May 14, 1951.)

But that was Cal. He was a prankster and a practical joker. And he had countless folksy sayings that he never minded repeating, which is why our family remembers them so well. When he died, on October 13, 2016, at age 90, my siblings texted one another their most memorable Cal quotes, which instantly brought back to our minds the rich uniqueness my uncle had contributed to our family. For example, if you found yourself riding down the road in his old green Chevy truck, he would frantically point to the pavement in front of us and say, "Look in the road—a head!" If you complained that your head hurt when you leaned over, Cal would say, "Then don't lean over." If anyone were looking for their glasses, he would say, "You can't look for your glasses until you find them."

The other thing I learned about my uncle was that he was not only named after President J. Calvin Coolidge, but he was related to him too. Cal was the 30th President's eighth cousin. At the back of this book, I have included a newspaper article from 1930 entitled, "'Coolidge Clan' Gathers in Annual Reunion..." I think you will find the article interesting.

Also included in the artifacts was a book written by Emma Downing Coolidge, entitled *Descendants of John and Mary Coolidge of Watertown, Massachusetts 1630*. In brief, John and Mary Coolidge traveled from England to America in 1630 during the second wave of those first American Colonists. President J. Calvin Coolidge was a descendant of John and Mary's second son; my family descends from their eldest son—"Ensign" John Coolidge.

A longer explanation of our genealogy can be found at the back of this book under "notes," but as stated on page 51 of Emma Coolidge's book, eventually we read that Harry Lyman Coolidge married Lillie B. Pierce. They had two children—my grandfather, Franklin Pierce Coolidge, born on October 9, 1898, in Athol, Massachusetts, and my Aunt Ellen. Franklin married Doris Elizabeth Nesbit, who was born on August 29, 1907, in Westfield, Massachusetts. Franklin and Doris had two children—my uncle, John Calvin Coolidge, born on April 24,

1926, and my mother, Ann Nesbit Coolidge, born on February 18, 1929, the year of the great stock market crash.

Though I go by Lisa, my birth name is Elizabeth Ann. I was named after my grandmother, Doris "Elizabeth," and my mother, "Ann." I did not learn of my legal name until the first day of Kindergarten class. The teacher called out "Elizabeth Soland" and I looked around the room wondering who had my last name. I was sixth out of the seven Soland children. My grandmother, Doris, and grandfather, Franklin, were my godparents.

I found this story so compelling because of the juxtaposition of events involving my uncle, Calvin, my mother, Ann, and my father, Norman.

J. Calvin Coolidge entered the Army on September 26, 1950, while his sister Ann (my mother), was studying to be a nurse at the New England Baptist Hospital, School of Nursing. My Uncle Cal was wounded in North Korea during the battle of King's Hill at the same time my mother was attending her formal graduation exercises. After my father returned from participating in The Berlin Airlift, he and my mother met. I recently asked him what his exact job was during that critical counter to the Berlin blockade. He responded, "It was my job to make sure the planes flew." My parents were married on December 28, 1951, just three weeks after they met, and soon after, Norman swept her off to Ladd Air Force Base in Alaska. They had just missed seeing Calvin in Camp Stoneman, Pittsburg, California, on their way to Alaska and his way back to the states from Korea.

In the Korean War, my uncle Cal served as a 57-mm recoilless rifle squad leader with the 32nd Infantry Regiment, 7th Infantry Division. He received the Korean Service Ribbon with two stars, which meant he fought in two major Korean War campaigns. Calvin also received the Presidential Unit Citation Emblem, the Combat Infantryman Badge, and the Purple Heart. He was wounded on Hill 902 during the battle of King's Hill. Following his recovery, Cal was transported back to the front lines, where he spent ten weeks fighting in the famous battle of Heartbreak Ridge. He reached the rank of Corporal before being released.

My father, Norman, has just turned 95. He lives in a veteran's facility, having served in the United States Air Force for 20 years. I can't think of a more respectful way to honor him and my mother for their years of service (and for raising seven children) than to place this book into their hands. I want to also thank my parents for remembering essential details that took place during this uncertain time in their lives (and American history). I am also grateful for my uncle's wife, Aunt Christy, who helped in the same manner. While preparing the New Salem estate for sale, Christy set Calvin's wartime letters aside for me. When I joined her in the task, we discovered decades of old family journals, photographs, newspaper clippings, and other artifacts that the Coolidge family had saved for generations.

Each letter has been transcribed without revision. No spelling or punctuation errors have been fixed in order to present the works as originally penned. Occasional corrections have been inserted using brackets for clarity purposes only. Capturing the language as initially executed offers a clearer portrayal of the writer's personality, mindset, and environment. It is my hope that these artifacts alone tell the story. I have been honored to play a role in bringing their experiences, feelings, and values back to the forefront of whatever public is drawn to enjoy them.

Like the times depicted in *J. Calvin Coolidge: Letters from the Korean War*, today we too face uncertainty. As I write this introduction, our world is struggling to recover from two years of the Covid-19 pandemic, which contributed to thousands of business closures and a strained economy that continues to impact us all. There are also concerns about possible food shortages that could expand across the globe. And now the Russian government has seen it necessary to invade Ukraine, making the pages of this book even more timely.

The Korean War began on June 25, 1950, when the North Korean Communist army crossed the 38th Parallel and invaded non-Communist South Korea. As I pieced together the puzzle of their intertwining stories, I watched Calvin, Ann, and Norman navigate their way through the years of the Korean War. May this account of my family's heritage be a gentle reminder that life is hard, but those who persist and forge through the difficulties come out victorious. Each of their stories deserves to be told. It is my hope that these words, *their words*, inspire you as they have me.

Lisa Soland, Senior Editor
Climbing Angel Publishing
April 2022
Knoxville, Tennessee

Seven children:

1. Louisa, b. about 1835; m. Jan. 4, 1854, ALBERT A. HANSON of New Salem, b. at Prescott.
2. Henry H., blacksmith, b. about 1837; m. (1st) June 20, 1860, JENNIE COLLORE of Wendell; two sons; m. (2d), June 20, 1900, MARY B. (PERRY) RICH, dau. of Charles and Mary (Peckham).
   1. Frank, b. about 1865; m. May 29, 1897, DELLA L. MARTIN, b. at Moores, N. Y., dau. of Richard and Mary (Hamlin).
   2. Fred, b. about 1871; m. Oct. 22, 1891, ROSE A. LE HERRISIER of Boston, b. at Newport, Vt., dau. of Peter and Constance.
3. Charles Pierce, b. about 1838; m. Nov. 23, 1864, EMMA CORDELIA UPTON, b. about 1847. He was a talented musician, and maker of violins as a hobby.
   Two children:
   1. George A., b. Sept. 8, 1867; m. Dec. 20, 1888, ALICE G. BRAGG, dau. of Greenleaf and Ophelia of Bangor, Me.
   2. Charles Eugene, pattern-maker, b. Oct. 8, 1874; m. June 7, 1897, ANNIE LOUISE HERRICK, b. about 1876, dau. of John and Louisa (Mayo). He was instructor of manual training at Orange High School.
      Two children:
      1. Adalia Christelle, b. Dec. 22, 1900.
      2. Arlan Ralph, b. Apr. 10, 1902. Grad. Brown University and a talented violinist, evidently inheriting his grandfather's aptitude.
4. Benjamin Franklin, b. Oct. 19, 1841; d. Aug. 24, 1876; m. June 13, 1867, DOROTHY ADELINE JONES, dau. of Rev. Nelson B. and Lucy (Glazier), b. Nov. 24, 1843, d. July 31, 1916.
   Their son, Harry Lyman, b. at New Salem, Dec. 14, 1870; m. Jan. 12, 1897, LILLIE B. PIERCE, dau. of Daniel and Ellen of Prescott.
   Two children:
   1. Franklin Pierce, b. Oct. 9, 1898; m. Dec. 2, 1925, DORIS ELIZABETH NESBIT, b. about 1907, dau. of Thomas W. and Ida (Brazee) of Westfield. They had a son John Calvin, b. at Athol, 1926. Reside at Holyoke.
   2. Ellen Adeline, b. May 26, 1906.
5. George Oscar, b. Nov. 17, 1844.
6. Susan, b. June 25, 1848; for years a very successful teacher; m. Oct. 6, 1885, JOHN PACKETT, son of Lewis and Rose of Montreal, Can.
7. Jennie, b. Oct. 13, 1851.

(Page 51 from the book *Descendants of John and Mary Coolidge of Watertown, Massachusetts 1630*, by Emma Downing Coolidge.)

Looking

Looking up I see the sky,
Looking down green grasses lie,
And between are trees and flowers–
God's and ours.

– J. Calvin Coolidge

(Harry Lyman Coolidge, their son Franklin Pierce Coolidge, and Harry's wife Lillie Pierce Coolidge. Franklin was Calvin and Ann's father.)

(Lillie, Franklin, Ellen Adeline, and Harry Coolidge.)

(Sisters: Mabel, Doris, and Ruth Nesbit.
Doris “Nesbit” Coolidge was Calvin and Ann’s mother.)

(Franklin and Doris Elizabeth "Nesbit" Coolidge, Calvin & Ann's father and mother.)

(John Calvin Coolidge's baby picture.)

(Franklin and Doris Coolidge,
with their children, Calvin and Ann.)

(Doris and Franklin, with Calvin and Ann.)

(Back row, from left to right: Leslie Pierce [Lillie's brother] Franklin Coolidge in car, Harry Coolidge. Middle row: Bertha Pierce [Leslie's wife], Lillie Coolidge, Jennie Shaw, [member of the Prescott Historical Society] and Doris Coolidge. Sitting on the ground in front: Calvin and Ann Coolidge.)

[A poem by Calvin. The envelope reads, "to my Dear mother."]

To my mother:

Hundreds of stars in the sky;
  Hundreds of shells on the shore together;
Hundreds of birds that go singing by;
  Hundreds of bees in the sunny weather.

Hundreds of dewdrops to greet the dawn;
  Hundreds of lambs in the purple clover;
Hundreds of butterflies on the lawn;
  But only one mother the wide world over.

Calvin

(A young Calvin might have been inspired to draw by his Aunt Ellen who was an artist, amongst other things. She loved to paint. Above, "Washington at Valley Forge," by Calvin Coolidge. To the left, his Aunt Ellen painting her annual Christmas card.)

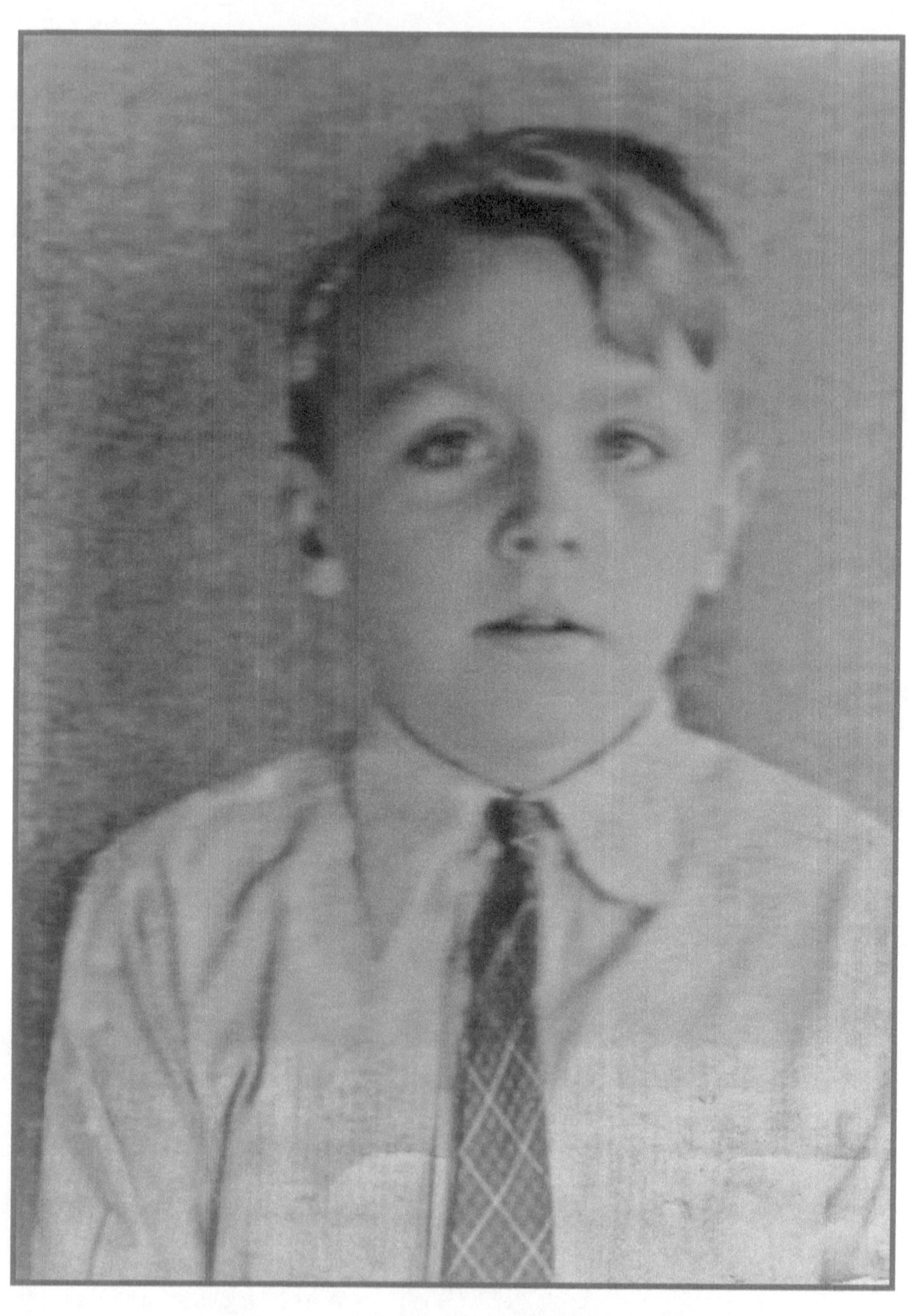

(John Calvin Coolidge, born in Athol, Massachusetts, on April 24, 1926.)

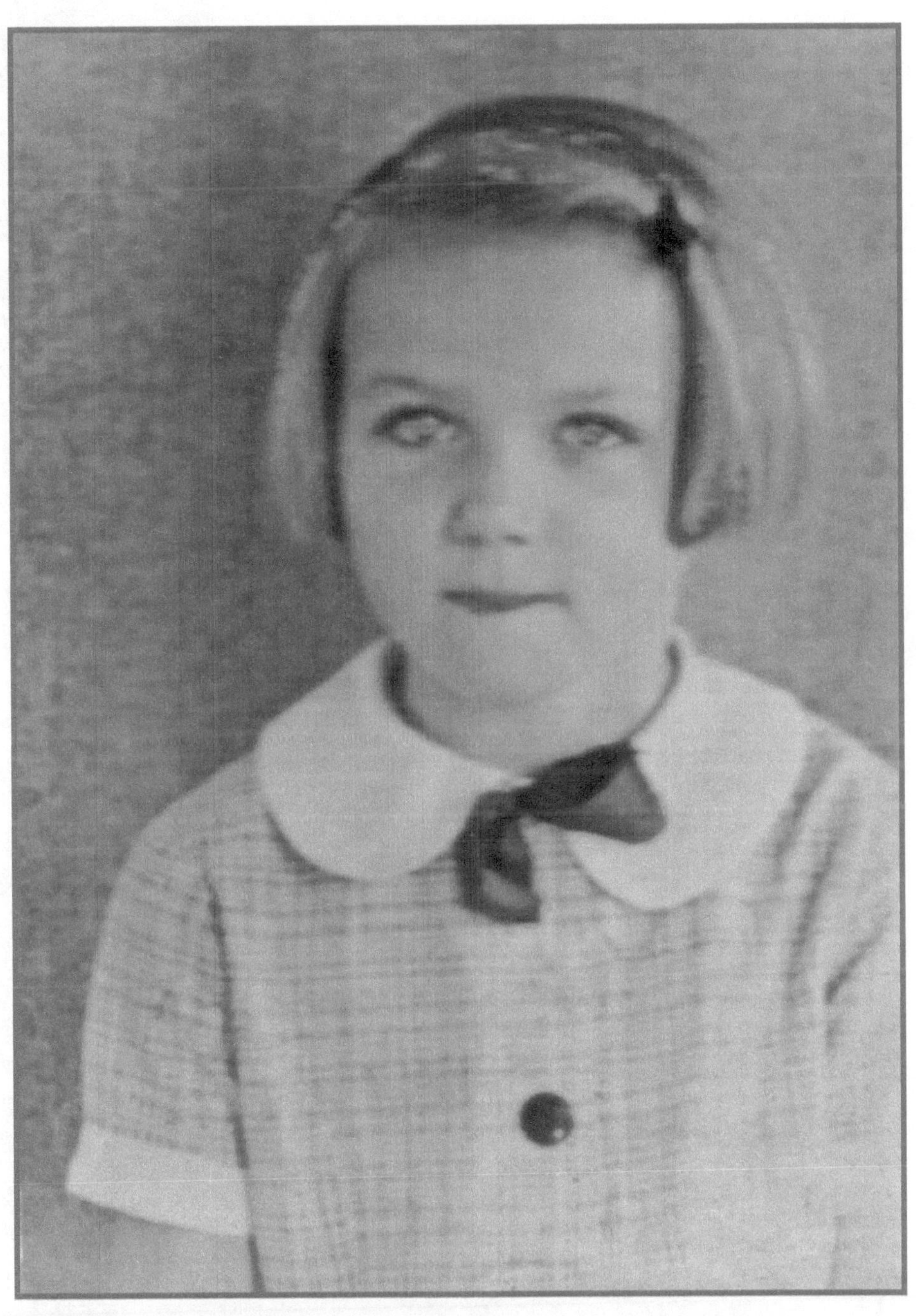

(Ann Nesbit Coolidge, born in Westfield, Massachusetts, on February 18, 1929.)

(The top drawing was created by a young Calvin Coolidge, and the bottom by his Aunt, Ellen Coolidge.)

(A young Ann and Calvin posing for their grandparents and Aunt Ellen at 11 Coolidge Drive, New Salem.)

(Ann and Calvin at their grandparent's home,
Harry and Lillie Coolidge.)

NAME Calvin Coolidge

SCHOLARSHIP AND CITIZENSHIP RECORD

SUBJECTS	SEPT. OCT.	NOV. DEC.	JAN. FEB.	MARCH APRIL	MAY JUNE	FINAL MARK	HIGH SCHOOL POINTS EARNED
Citizenship	A	A	A	A	a	a	1
Days Absent	1	0	0	0	0	1	
Times Tardy	0	0	0	0	0	0	
Dismissals	0	0	0	0	0	0	
ENGLISH	C X3	X3	X	X3	B c	C+	5
Reading or Literature							
Composition							
Grammar or Language							
Penmanship							
Public Speaking							
Spelling							
Lip Reading							
MATHEMATICS							
1.							
2.							
SOCIAL STUDIES							
Civics							
History	C-2	C-2	C-2	B-1	A1	B-1	5
Geography							
~~Occupation~~ Guidance	C-2	A-2	C-2	C-3	C-2	C	2
FOREIGN LANGUAGES							
French							
Latin							
SCIENCE							
1.							
AGRICULTURE	A1/A1	A1/A1	B1/B1	a/a	a/a	a	5
COMMERCIAL							
1.							
2.							
3.							
FINE ARTS							
Drawing							
Music							
PHYSICAL EDUCATION			B-1	C-1	B-1	B-1	1¼
PRACTICAL ARTS							
1.							
2.							
3.							
PROSPECT OF PROMOTION	**** ****	**** ****			**** ****	TOTAL	

Grade 12 Room Pa.T. Teacher H. F. Bartlett

EXPLANATION OF MARKING SYSTEM

SCHOLARSHIP

A=90-100%	Excellent	College Certificate Grades (High School).
B=80-90%	Good	
C=70-79%	Fair	Passing.
X=67-69%	Unsatisfactory	Warning of No Promotion in subject.
F=60-67%	Failure	Conference desired.
Z=0-60%	Complete Failure	Not adapted to subject.
I=	Incomplete	Make up the work.

The mark in each subject consists of a letter and figure. The letter indicates achievement and the figure the pupil's attitude toward work. Ratings of X, F, or 4 indicate the need for a conference between the parent and the teacher. (Explanation for attitude marks will be found on page 4). Any mark below B is unsatisfactory for citizenship. If there are two marks given, the second mark shows whether pupil is improving or getting worse.

(A) HIGH HONORS: Averages A on written work.
Penmanship legible.
Spelling excellent.
Recitations show superior grasp of subject.
Work done on time

(B) HONORS— Written work averages B
Spelling good.
Penmanship legible.
Recitations show good grasp of subject.
Work usually done on time.

(C) AVERAGE— Written work averages C
Spelling and Penmanship usually satisfactory.
Recitations show slowness to grasp subject.
Work often done on time.

(X) WARNING— Oral and written work doubtful.
Marks vary from day to day.
Tests often failed.
Careless in spelling and penmanship.
Attitude marks may show problem.
Work seldom done on time.

(F) FAILURE— Oral and written work poor, varies too much.
Tests usually failed.
Spelling and penmanship poor.
Work rarely done on time.

(Z) COMPLETE FAILURE—Oral and written work shows lack of preparation.
Tests failed regularly.
Spelling and penmanship unsatisfactory.
Work never done on time.

(One of Calvin's report cards from his senior year in High School. As you can see, he excelled in citizenship and his agricultural course where he served as secretary for the West Springfield branch of Future Farmers of America.)

(J. Calvin Coolidge's High School Graduation Picture, 1943.)

THE SIXTY-EIGHTH
ANNUAL

GRADUATION EXERCISES

OF THE

WEST SPRINGFIELD HIGH SCHOOL

MONDAY EVENING
JUNE 21, 1943

(Calvin's Graduation Exercises of the West Springfield High School program, dated June 21, 1943, four pages total.)

There Was A Dream

THERE was a dream* . . . that men could one day speak the thoughts of their own choosing.—There was a hope . . . that men could one day stroll through streets at evening, unafraid.—There was a prayer . . . that each could speak to his own God—in his own church—That dream, that hope, that prayer became . . . America!—Great strength, youthful heart, vast enterprise, hard work made it so.—Now that same America is the dream . . . the hope . . . the prayer of the world.—Our freedom—its dream Our strength—its hope.—Our swift race against time—its prayer!—We must not fail the world now. We must not fail to share our freedom with it—afterwards . . . *Keep Singing, Keep Working, and Fight for America!*

*Reproduced by Courtesy of E. R. Squibb & Sons

Class Song

We are the class of '43;
Together we will stand,
Our goal a world of joyous freedom
Peace in every land.
We have the spirit for our guide
Of our democracy;
Victorious and glorious
Our purpose will ever be.

We are the class of '43;
With hearts and spirits high,
Our faith in victory never wavers,
There our futures lie.
Now we go out to put an end
To hate and fear and war
That strife may cease and lasting peace
Be with us forever more.

A Mighty Fortress

A mighty fortress is our God, a bulwark never failing;
Our helper He, amid the flood of mortal ills prevailing.
For still our ancient foe doth seek to work us woe;
His craft and pow'r are great, and, armed with cruel hate,
On earth is not His equal.

That word above all earthly powers, no thanks to them abideth:
The Spirit and the gifts are ours through Him who with us sideth:
Let goods and kindred go, this mortal life also;
The body they may kill; God's truth abideth still,
His kingdom is for ever.

Certificates of Work Completed

Shirlie Ruth Aldrich
*Donald Bishop
Henrica Bobbe
John J. Cain
J. Calvin Coolidge
*Thomas Corbett
Betty Jane Costine
*Nicholas Delnero
*Walter Fiala
Nando Fontana
Mary Galiatsos
*Larry Gamsby
Carmela Yolanda Grimaldi
Rose Mary Grimaldi
*Frederick Hartwell
Minnie Helen Henderson
Shirley E. Hodge
Richard E. Hogan
Duane Harold Jones
*Theron Luce
Virginia Laurianne Maheu
*Vincent Marceno
Ellen McGarrett
*John Mergerian
Shirley J. Morse
Gladys Helen Nevers
Robert R. O'Connell
Wallace E. Orr
Marguerite Lorraine Parent
*Floyd Perkins
Allyn Frank Prochaska
Dorothy Mary Rosner
Claire M. Russell
Joseph W. Russell, Jr.
Frank R. Salvadori
Kenneth D. Schroeter
William E. Taylor
*Edward Voyik
Chester Frank Warren

*In the Service

COOLIDGE WINS $25 WAR BOND [2/5/44]

Youth One of Six State Visitors in Contest

Through his accuracy in examinations and his reports of practical gardening, John Calvin Coolidge of 1537 Riverdale Street, West Springfield, has won a $25 war bond in a scholarship contest sponsored by the National Junior Vegetable Growers Association.

One of Six Winners

One of six Massachusetts entrants to come through in the national contest out of 29 entered from the state, Coolidge is a student at the Stockbridge School of Agriculture in Amherst. He took a correspondence course given by Prof. Grant B. Snyder of Massachusetts State College and answered questions on the information, along with forwarding records of his gardening and other projects in agriculture.

He has worked at local market gardens, was secretary of the West Springfield local of Future Farmers of America, and was a member of the vocational agriculture judging team for 1941 and 1942. He studied vocational agriculture at the local schools under the direction of Herbert F. Bartlett, and was awarded the Chamber of Commerce prize during the high school graduation last June.

At the state FFA meeting in Worcester Jan. 28, he was elected reporter for the state association. He was also one of 10 nominated by the executive board for the Bay State Farmer Degree, an advanced degree of the FFA.

He is the 17-years-old son of Mr. and Mrs. Franklin Pierce Coolidge, with whom he is spending the weekend. His records showed aa profit of $93.82 on the 10,000 square foot garden he planted last season.

CALVIN COOLIDGE LEAVES FOR SCHOOL

J. Calvin Coolidge, 17, son of Mr. and Mrs. Franklin Coolidge of 1537 Riverdale Street, left yesterday to enter Stockbridge School at Amherst. The fact is of unusual interest to West Springfield residents, who have followed his farming career for several years. He was graduated from West Springfield High School last June, where he took the agricultural course and served as secretary of the Future Farmers of America. He found time to supplement his studies with a great deal of practical experience.

He assisted at Doty's market gardens, cared for stock on the Hay's farm and also maintained a home garden of one third of an acre that not only provided food for his family during the summer but also for winter use. The sale of some of his excellent produce brought top prices. He will be able to finance his college course through his work.

Along with the customary garden crops, he has included enough potatoes for winter use and sufficient dry navy beans to last the entire winter. Carrots have been stored and parsnips were planted that will be ready for spring digging. After an outstanding yield of green beans had been gathered, he planted some bancroft corn July 4 and the family is now enjoying it. Mrs. Coolidge has been able to can from his garden approximately 400 jars of a variety of vegetables, in addition to pickles made from a large supply of cucumbers and tomatoes.

CALVIN COOLIDGE LEAVES FOR SCHOOL

J. Calvin Coolidge, 17, son of Mr. and Mrs. Franklin Coolidge of 1537 Riverdale Street, left yesterday to enter Stockbridge School at Amherst. The fact is of unusual interest to West Springfield residents, who have followed his farming career for several years. He was graduated from West Springfield High School last June, where he took the agricultural course and served as secretary of the Future Farmers of America. He found time to supplement his studies with a great deal of practical experience.

He assisted at Doty's market gardens, cared for stock on the Hay's farm and also maintained a home garden of one third of an acre that not only provided food for his family during the summer but also for winter use. The sale of some of his excellent produce brought top prices. He will be able to finance his college course through his work.

Along with the customary garden crops, he has included enough potatoes for winter use and sufficient dry navy beans to last the entire winter. Carrots have been stored and parsnips were planted that will be ready for spring digging. After an outstanding yield of green peas had been gathered, he planted some bancroft corn July 4 and the family is now enjoying it. Mrs. Coolidge has been able to can from his garden approximately 400 jars of a variety of vegetables, in addition to pickles made from a large supply of cucumbers and tomatoes.

STOCKBRIDGE SCHOOL
OF AGRICULTURE
MASSACHUSETTES STATE COLLEGE
AMHERST, MASS.

(The program of Calvin's graduation from Stockbridge School of Agriculture. Included are nine of the most pertinent pages.)

F O R E W O R D

When shady recollections of Stockbridge go

wandering through your heart, remove this

yearbook from its dusty nook and turn

each page with a careful hand so that

many old friends and pleasant memories

will be revealed to you once again.

The Editors

CLASS HISTORY

We wandered into Amherst from all directions to begin our studies in Stockbridge in the autumn of '43. Being the first class to graduate under the accelerated wartime program has been a history-making experience.

On September 27th all registered at the Short Course Office and classes began on the following day. New acquaintances were made and many lasting friendships have developed. The seasonal holidays marked the end of our first semester and all went home for two weeks.

Again we came to Amherst to resume our studies which began on January 3. The second semester saw the arrival of a veteran of the South Pacific in our midst. Time passed rapidly. The poultry students were the first to leave for their placement training and they were followed one month later by the remainder of Stockbridge men and women.

Our time at Stockbridge was well spent and has shown us a guiding light to the future.

CLASS OFFICERS

President . . . . Robert L. Thompson

Vice President . . . . James M. Scott

Secretary . . . . Virginia M. Oates

Treasurer . . . . Gilbert W. Nichols

SHORTHORN
1944

Cal is related to the late president in some way. Rather quiet, he is one of the Veg Gardening partners. It seemed as if he resided with Joe Ely most of the time. He always enjoyed a good argument. He was also a very good student, standing first or second in his class. No wonder, there were only two members in his class most of the time.

John Calvin Coolidge
West Springfield, Mass.

Between the Holyoke and local girls Joe was kept pretty busy. That may explain the appearance of the flashy coupe which could be seen travelling from class to class on the campus. Although girls seemed to be his pet avocation he always managed to keep in front in his Vegetable Gardening work. Possessing a pleasing personality and exceedingly quick wit which was used to good advantage, he always had but one big worry, gas stamps. However, with his practical training and sound judgment we are certain that this ambitious gentleman will go far towards being one of our leading Vegetable Gardeners.

Joseph Houston Ely
Holyoke, Mass.

20

(My uncle, J. Calvin Coolidge, was named after the 30th President of the United States, and was the President's 8th cousin.)

TO THE STUDENTS OF THE STOCKBRIDGE SCHOOL OF AGRICULTURE:

My hearty congratulations go to you who have completed your training for service which will be of invaluable aid to the Allied armies now fighting for victory.

It is said often that food will win the war and write the peace. In contributing to the efficient and speedy production of food, each of you is aiding directly our final victory. The army on the production line in the factories, and the army producing food are equally important in our battle for the final defeat of the Axis.

You are to be congratulated for taking your place in the food production army, for you can look for no spectacular service, no medals for bravery, there. But your heroism and self-sacrifice will mean just as much to the success of the allied armies in this war as the heroic deeds of our young men and women overseas in the battle area.

We wish you good luck and Godspeed, as you go out to take your place in the important wartime work of agriculture. Yours is an important responsibility, and we feel confident that you will meet successfully the challenge of our nation at war.

Hugh P. Baker, President
Massachusetts State College

THE WAR AND YOUR SCHOOL

The school year 1943-44 finds Stockbridge, like all other schools and colleges, facing the stern realities of the greatest war in history. Radical changes have had to be made in the school program to make possible even the smallest enrolments in agriculture. Several of our major courses have no students registered and have been temporarily cancelled, such as Dairy Manufactures, Hotel Stewarding, and Fruit Growing.

Early last year it was seen these changes would be inevitable, and the administration and faculty recommended the one year war emergency program we have now adopted, lowering the entering age from seventeen to sixteen years. Fall term registration brought fourteen new students in Animal Husbandry, four for Poultry, three for Vegetable Gardening, and five for a combined course in Horticulture and Floriculture, since neither of these could be given singly. After completing two twelve week terms of classes all students will immediately take farm jobs for placement, and if this six months work is completed creditably, certificates, not the usual two-year diploma, will be mailed to them. This means no formal graduation or any of the usual school activities, such as dances and athletic teams, are now possible. Stockbridge is on a strictly war basis for the duration, hoping to be able to keep its facilities in working shape for its present student body, giving them the best we have, and ready to expand and restore the old program once peace is declared. We are sure there will be ample need then for everything we can give when our soldier-farmers coming marching home.

A brief summary of Stockbridge registration shows how the war has curtailed our numbers.

Registration 1941	Second year - 105	First Year - 110	Total - 215
Registration 1942	Second Year - 59	First Year - 71	Total - 130
Registration 1943	Second Year - None	First Year - 27	Total - 27

To the students of the one year class of 1944 we extend our sincere well-wishes for the future. You are doing your essential part in food production as a war contribution, difficult as it is to stay on the farm. Even though your numbers are small, you, too, have played an important part in the life of Stockbridge, a part you and I will not soon forget. We appreciate your spirit and loyalty in keeping alive the custom of a school yearbook as a record of this year at Massachusetts State College.

Roland H. Verbeck
Director of Short Courses

THE FACULTY

Doric Alviani, M.Ed.	Instructor in Music
Luther Banta, B.S.	Assistant Professor of Poultry Husbandry
Rollin H. Barrett, M.S.	Professor of Farm Management
Lyle L. Blundell, B.S.	Professor of Horticulture
Lawrence S. Dickinson, M.S.	Assistant Professor of Agrostology
Guy V. Glatfelter, M.S.	Acting Head of Placement Service
Francis P. Griffiths, Ph.D.	Professor of Horticultural Manufactures and Acting Head of Department
Margaret P. Hamlin, B.S.	Placement Officer for Women
Marshall C. Heck, M.S.	Assistant Professor of Animal Husbandry
S. Church Hubbard	Assistant Professor of Floriculture
William H. Lachman, M.S.	Instructor in Vegetable Gardening
John B. Lentz, A.B., V.M.D.	Professor of Veterinary Science and Head of Department
Harry G. Lindquist, M.S.	Assistant Professor of Dairying
John B. Newlon	Instructor in Agricultural Engineering
Raymond T. Parkhurst, Ph.D.	Professor of Poultry Husbandry and Head of Department
Clarence H. Parsons, M.S.	Assistant Professor of Animal Husbandry and Superintendent of Farm
George F. Pushee	Instructor in Agricultural Engineering
Victor A. Rice, M.Agr.	Professor of Animal Husbandry and Head of Department, Head of Division of Agriculture
Oliver C. Roberts, M.S.	Assistant Professor of Pomology
Donald E. Ross, B.S.	Instructor in Floriculture and Greenhouse Foreman
William C. Sanctuary, M.S.	Professor of Poultry Husbandry
Samuel P. Snow, B.L.A.	Instructor in Horticulture
Grant B. Snyder, M.S.	Professor of Vegetable Gardening and Head of Department
William H. Tague, B.S.	Assistant Professor of Agricultural Engineering
Charles H. Thayer	Assistant Professor of Agronomy
Clark L. Thayer, B.S.	Professor of Floriculture and Head of Department
Alden P. Tuttle, M.S.	Assistant Professor of Vegetable Gardening
John H. Vondell	Assistant Professor of Poultry Husbandry
Lowell E. Walters, M.S.	Assistant Professor of Animal Husbandry
Karl W. Woodward, M.F.	Instructor in Forestry

CLASS OF 1944

ANIMAL HUSBANDRY

Bisbee, William Homer
Chesterfield
Buchanan, Thomas Sampers
Sharon, Conn.
Burt, Herschel Bacon
Weston
Clapp, David George
Westhampton
Hamill, Creighton
Holyoke
Mason, Thomas Adam
Swansea
Nichols, Gilbert White
Grafton
Patenaude, Wayne Clifford
Hopedale

Pearson, Erick Birger
Worcester
Roberts, Arthur Wellsley
Malden
Shattuck, Leon Richard
East Pepperell
Siegel, Irving Morris
Columbia, Conn.
Thompson, Robert Lewis
East Braintree
Thouin, Robert Hector
Northampton
Tobin, Thomas Theodore
Springfield

POULTRY HUSBANDRY

Bolin, Donald Raymond
Milford
Driscoll, Frederick David
Beverly

Hayward, Allen Clifton
Halifax
Lyon, Norman Josiah
Ludlow
Scott, James Michael
Weymouth

ORNAMENTAL HORTICULTURE

Davis, Donald William
North Abington
Lima, Antone Vincent
Vineyard Haven
Madison, Luther Tachnash, Jr.
Gay Head

Oates, Virginia Mae
Shelburne Falls
Sullivan, Jane Beckett
Egypt

VEGETABLE GARDENING

Coolidge, John Calvin
West Springfield

Schofield, Bernard Anthony
South Sudbury

Ely, Joseph Houston
Holyoke

SPECIAL STUDENTS

John Joseph O'Brien
Winthrop
Donald Prouty Young
Boylston

GRADUATES - CLASS OF 1944

William Homer Bisbee	Chesterfield, Massachusetts
Donald Raymond Bolin	Milford, Massachusetts
Thomas Sampers Buchanan	Sharon, Connecticut
Herschel Bacon Burt	Weston, Massachusetts
David George Clapp	Westhampton, Massachusetts
John Calvin Coolidge	West Springfield, Massachusetts
Frederick David Driscoll	Beverly, Massachusetts
Norman Josiah Lyon	Ludlow, Massachusetts
Luther Tachnash Madison, Jr.	Gay Head, Massachusetts
Thomas Adam Mason	Swansea, Massachusetts
Gilbert White Nichols	Grafton, Massachusetts
Virginia Mae Oates	Shelburne Falls, Massachusotts
Wayne Clifford Patenaude	Hopedale, Massachusetts
Leon Richard Shattuck	East Pepperell, Massachusetts
Irving Morris Siegal	Columbia, Connecticut
Robert Lewis Thompson	East Braintree, Massachusetts
Robert Hector Thouin	Northampton, Massachusetts

This is the first class to graduate under the new one year plan to meet the war emergency for farm labor in food production. The entering age for Stockbridge students has been lowered from seventeen to sixteen years, and the school year consists only of two 12-week terms of classes from October to December and from January to March, followed by the usual six months placement training on jobs. On the satisfactory completion of all class and placement requirements students are awarded new one year certificates, 8" x 6", inserted in navy blue leather folders, inscribed in gold with the state seal and "Stockbridge School of Agriculture." No formal graduation takes place and all certificates are mailed to students in December after placement reports have been checked and grades evaluated.

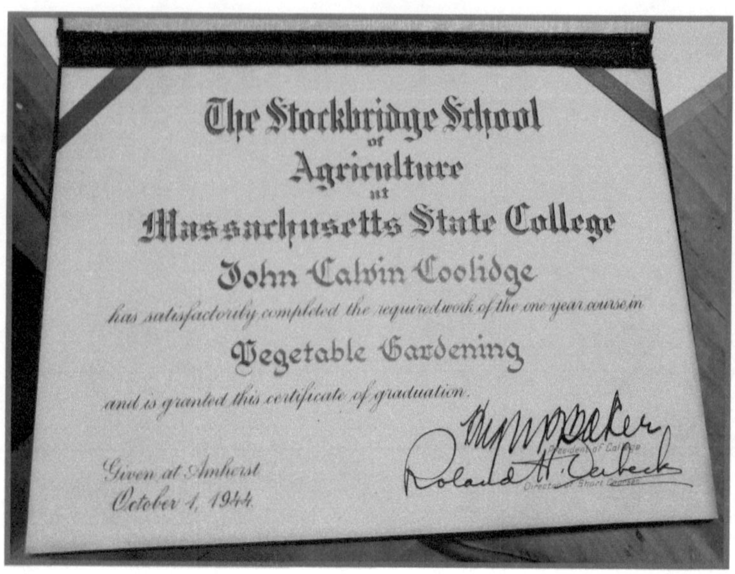

The Stockbridge School of Agriculture at Massachusetts State College

John Calvin Coolidge

has satisfactorily completed the required work of the one year course in

Vegetable Gardening

and is granted this certificate of graduation.

Given at Amherst
October 4, 1944

President of College

Director of Short Courses

(ABOVE: Calvin's certificate of graduation from The Stockbridge School of Agriculture on October 4, 1944. BELOW: A letter to Ann notifying her that she had been chosen the "Good Citizen" of her school.)

90 Maple St.
Springfield, Mass.
March 15, 1947

Dear Miss Coolidge [Ann]:

Mercy Warren Chapter of the Daughters of the American Revolution, is very happy to know you have been chosen the Good Citizen of your school.

In the name of Mercy Warren Chapter our regent, Mrs. Fred C. Brigham, wishes to extend to you an invitation to our next meeting to be held Monday, April 7, 1947, at two o'clock at the Springfield Women's Club House, Spring St., Springfield, Mass.

The meeting will include a program of American Classics and tea will be served.

We will be pleased to have you bring your mother or one relative who will also be our guest.

Will you please let me know if you will be able to attend this meeting?

We look forward with great pleasure to meeting you.

Cordially yours, Perses Hazen, Mrs. J. E. Hazen
Chapter Chairman, D.A,R. Citizenship Pilgrimage

(This photo was taken on Easter Sunday, April 21, 1946, at the Coolidge residence on Riverdale Road in West Springfield, Massachusetts. Ann Coolidge was 17 years old and in High School. Calvin was 20.)

(Ann Coolidge enjoyed skating and baton twirling.
This photo was taken in April of 1947.)

(Ann Coolidge's High School Graduation Picture, 1947.)

Classmates Enter Nursing Schools

Two West Springfield Girls Leave This Month

Miss Ann Coolidge, daughter of Mr. and Mr. Franklyn P. Coolidge of Riverdale St., West Springfield, and Miss Edith Dorian, daughter of Mr. and Mrs. Charles J. Dorian of Wayside Ave., West Sspringfield, former classmates at West Springfield High School, who were graduated with the 1947 class, are to enter nurses' training schools this month. Miss Coolidge is going to the New England Baptist Hospital in Boston and Miss Dorian will begin her studies at the Massachusetts General Hospital in that city.

At graduation exercises Miss Coolidge received the Latin and mathematics award, the Parent-Teacher Association scholarship, and was the winner of the DAR Good Citizenship Pilgrimage award for dependability, service, leadership and patriotism. She also was chosen Girls' State representative in her junior year ,and served the organization as treasurer. She also was treasurer of the Student Government, a majorette in the High School Band, a pro merito student, a member of the Glee Club and Student Patrol and student representative of the Assembly committee.

Miss Dorian was secretary of the Student Council, a member of the Glee Club, Student Patrol, Sock and Buskin and was on the staff of the year book. She served as cheer leader at soccer games, participated in the Valley Wheel oratorical contest and was also a pro merito student. This month she will complete a course of study at Springfield Junior College.

MISS ANN COOLIDGE

MISS EDITH DORIAN

ENTER NURSING SCHOOLS—Two West Springfield girls, graduates in the 1947 class of the high school, there, are to enter nurses' training school this month. They are Miss Ann Coolidge, daughter of Mr. and Mrs. Franklyn P. Coolidge of Riverdale Rd., and Miss Edith Dorian, daughter of Mr. and Mrs. Charles J. Dorian of Wayside Ave. Miss Coolidge is enrolled at the New England Baptist Hospital in Boston, and Miss Dorian has been accepted by the Massachusetts General Hospital.

"At graduation exercises Miss Coolidge received the Latin and mathematics award, the Parent-Teacher Association scholarship, and was the winner of the DAR Good Citizenship Pilgrimage award for dependability, service, leadership and patriotism. She also was chosen Girls' State representative in her junior year, and served the organization as treasurer. She also was treasurer of the Student Government, a majorette in the High School Band, a pro merito student, a member of the Glee Club and Student Patrol and student representative of the Assembly committee."

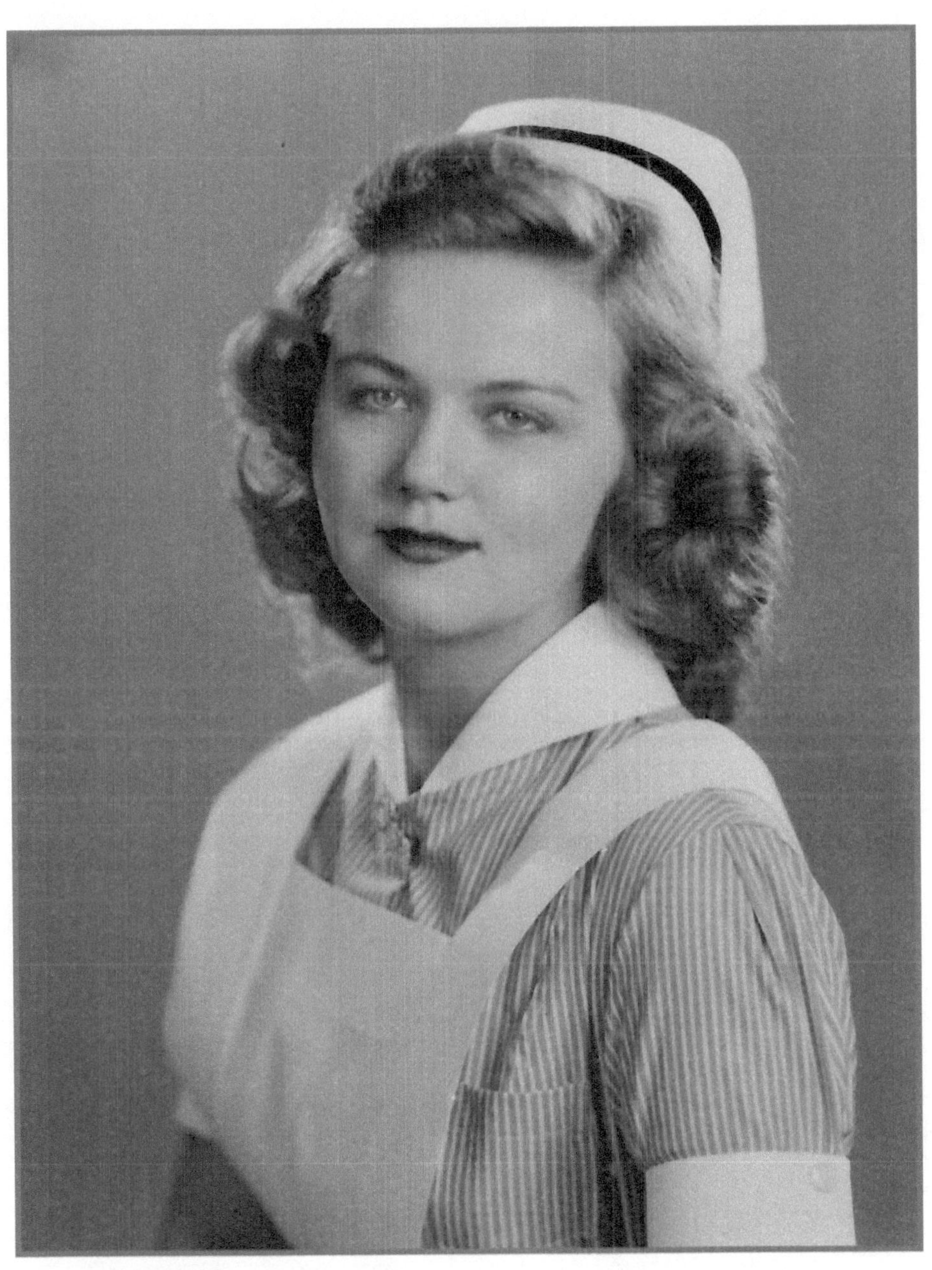

(This photo was taken of Ann Coolidge during Capping Exercises.)

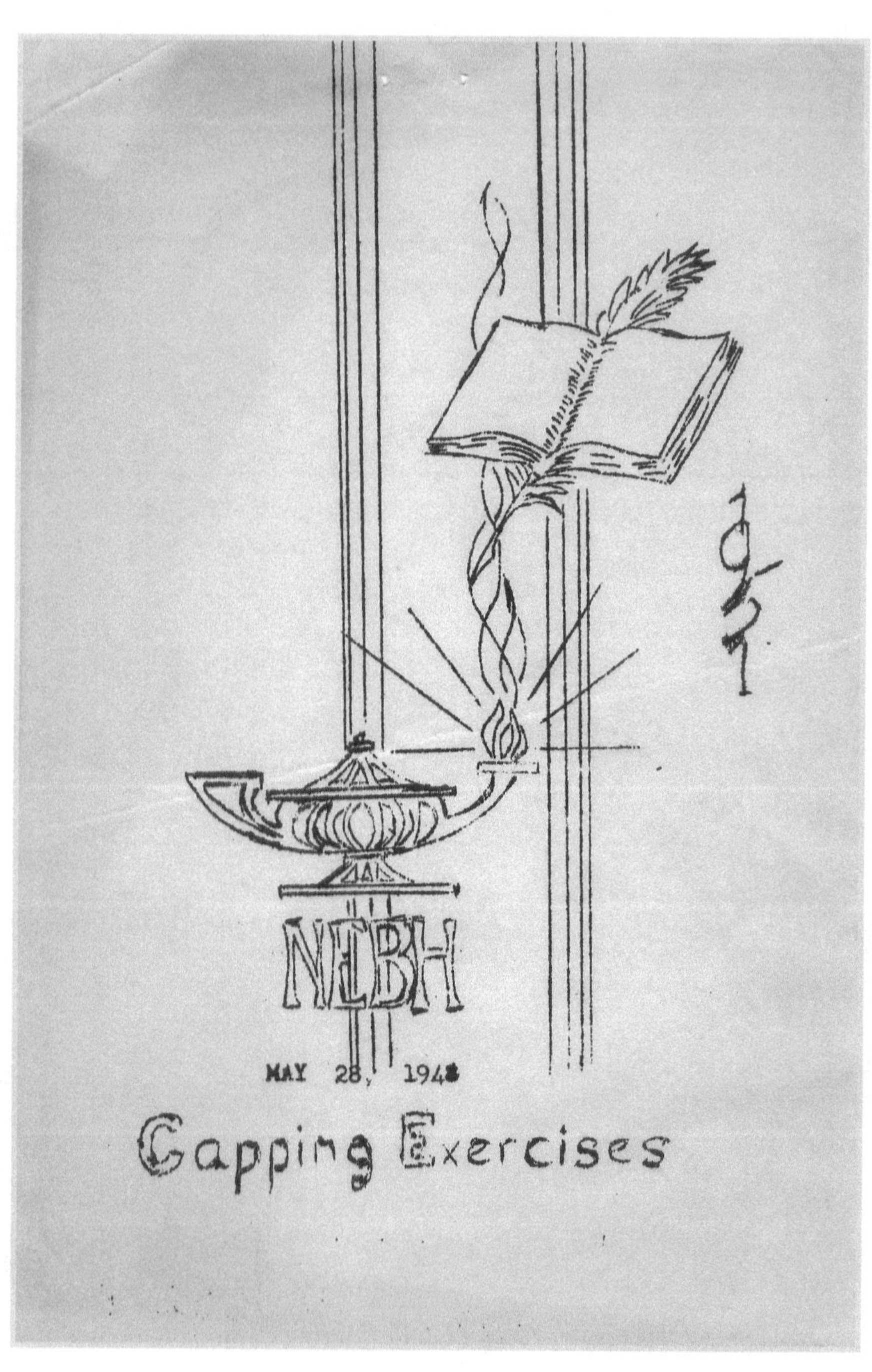

(Ann Coolidge's Capping Exercises Program, dated May 28, 1948, a total of seven pages.)

The holiest task by Heaven decreed,
An errand all divine,
The burden of our common need
To render less, is thine.

Beside the unveiled mysteries
Of life and death go stand,
With guarded lips and reverent eyes,
And pure of heart and hand.

—J. G. Whittier.

(Page 2 of the Capping Exercise Program.)

WEST SPRINGFIELD

SCHOLARSHIP TO MISS COOLIDGE

Receives $100 From Parent Teacher Group

West Springfield, March 10—Mrs. Frank Hays of Riverdale St., president of the Parent-Teacher Scholar-Allen, town clerk, announced today. that because Frank Whitford, winner of last year's award, has joined the Navy, the sum will go to Anne Coolidge, winner of the $50 award. Runnerup Roger Sullivan, son of Mr. and Mrs. George W. Sullivan of Riverdale St., will recieve the $50 award given Miss Coolidge.

Sullivan is a student at the University of Maine, in a chemical engineering course, and he was on the dean's list last term. Miss Coolidge is a student nurse at the Baptist Hospital, Boston.

WE ask God, in whom we have implicit faith, to guide us:

TO instill in us a genuine, sympathetic interest in others; also a desire to relieve mental and physical suffering, because we believe that true happiness lies in the service of others:

TO help us to develope our potential abilities; to cultivate honesty, tolerance, sincerity and personal integrity; and to maintain and elevate the standards of our profession:

TO realize our place in this generation, and our responsibility in the building of a better world:

TO these ends we dedicate ourselves.

reprinted from
Garfield Memorial Hospital
School of Nursing
Class of 1946

CAPPING SERVICE
New England Baptist Hospital - School of Nursing
Friday, May 28, 1948 - 8:15 o'clock

PROGRAM

Our father's God to Thee
Author of Liberty, to Thee we sing;
Long may our land be bright
With Freedom's holy light; protect
Us by Thy might, great God, our King. Amen.

School Hymn
Welcome to Parents and Friends
Georgie M. Boulter, Superintendent, N.E.B.H.

Welcome — Ruth Sieswerda '48
Sec. Student Co-op. Govt. Assn.

Response — Lois Landers, Pre-Clinical Student

Songs — Student Glee Club
Green Cathedral — Carl Hahn
Let Us Have Peace — Ernest R. Ball
Mr. Donald L. Marshall, Conducting
Miss Charlotte Sawyer, Piano

Prayer — School

Capping of Students and
Lighting the Nightingale Lamps
Georgie M. Boulter, Superintendent, N.E.B.H.
Nellie H. Pekrul, Principal, School of Nursing

The Nightingale Pledge — Class 1951

Send Out Thy Light — Class 1951 and Glee Club
Follow The Gleam

Recessional

O Thou whose gracious hand was ever stretched out to heal the sick, and who has promised Thy blessing to all who minister in Thy name, grant Thy tenderest blessing to this house of healing and all who come within its walls. Be with us in our daily life, walk with us as Thou wast wont to walk with Thy disciples, comfort all, and heal the sick. Enlarge our hearts, O Lord, to their utmost extent to love Thee, strengthen our minds to grasp Thee in Thy fullness, and may we feel ourselves one in the unity of Thy sacred humanity. May our watchword be love, our desire Thy law, and may we realize here the beauty of Thy service.

Almighty God, Father of all mercies, we, thine unworthy servants, do give thee most humble and hearty thanks for all thy goodness and loving kindness to us, and to all men. We bless thee for our creation, preservation, and all the blessings of this life; but above all, for Thine inestimable love in the redemption of the world by our Lord, Jesus Christ; for the means of grace, and for the hope of glory. And, we beseech Thee, give us that due sense of all thy mercies, that our hearts may be unfeignedly thankful; and that we show forth Thy praise, not only with our lips, but in our lives, by giving up ourselves to Thy service, and by walking before Thee in holiness and righteousness all our days; through Jesus Christ our Lord, to whom, with Thee and the Holy Ghost, be all honour and glory, world without end. Amen.

Our Father, which art in Heaven, hallowed be Thy Name. Thy kingdom come. Thy will be done in earth, as it is in Heaven. Give us this day our daily bread. And forgive us our trespasses, As we forgive them that trespass against us. And lead us not into temptation; but deliver us from evil, for Thine is the Kingdom, the power, and the glory, for ever and ever. Amen.

SCHOOL HYMN

Radiant the flame
That lights thy lamp of Truth,
Glorious thy name
Resplendant from Youth,----
We'll honor and love thee,
Thy great name revere,
The call to serve thee
Lights our visions clear.
Baptist School of Nursing
Make us worthy of thee. Anne Haynes '45.
Music: "Land of Hope and Glory" - Elgar

FOLLOW THE GLEAM

To the knights in the days of old,
Keeping watch on the mountain heights,
Came a vision of Holy Grail and a voice
Thro' the waiting night. Follow, follow,
Follow the gleam, banners unfurled o'er
All the world, follow, follow, follow
The gleam of the Light that shall bring the dawn.

And we who would serve the King,
And loyally Him obey, in the consecrate
Silence know that the challenge still
Holds today. Follow, follow, follow the
Gleam, standards of worth o'er all the
Earth. Follow, follow, follow the Gleam
Of the light that shall bring the dawn.

CLASS OF FEBRUARY 1951

Coolidge, Ann Nesbit	West Springfield, Mass.
Ellis, Priscilla Collingwood	Plymouth, Mass.
Harvey, Emma Ida	Leominster, Mass.
Hasty, Dorothy Estelle	Cape Elizabeth, Maine
Hoar, Joanne	Millis, Mass.
Landers, Lois Ann	Lynn, Mass.
Langelier, Irene Rose	Rochester, N.H.
McCoy, Barbara Anne	Fall River, Mass.
Moore, Elizabeth Jean	Bath, Maine
Moses, Cynthia Anne	Bath, Maine
Pickard, Nancy Estelle	Chelmsford, Mass.
Smith, Dorothy Jane	Randolph, Mass.
Young, Marie	No. Pembroke, Mass.

(Page 7 of the Capping Exercises program.)

[During Ann Coolidge's student nurse training at New England Baptist Hospital in Boston, old Joe Kennedy Sr. was admitted as a patient. He had been suffering from severe stomach ulcers.

Ann recalls, "In the late 1940s, there were two wings to the hospital—one for ordinary folks and one for people who preferred, and could afford, a private room. President Roosevelt had appointed Joe Kennedy Sr. to serve as Ambassador to Great Britain, so he was well known. He didn't want a registered nurse because they were too old for him; he wanted a young one. The head nurse chose me to take care of him, I suppose, because of my ability to pay attention to detail.

"There were no waiting rooms for family members of those who had private rooms, so they had to wait in the hall. I remember his wife being there that day, Rose, and others, maybe the Kennedy brothers—Robert, Ted, and John F. Kennedy—but I don't recall for sure. It was a long time ago. His family was waiting in the hall to visit him, and I was in their father's room giving him a back rub. Back then, the nurses gave daily back rubs to the patients because they were bedridden for such long times. And while I was rubbing his back, old Joe turned around, put his arms around me, and hugged me in a tight squeeze. I was just a student nurse and scared to death."]

(Neighbor Robert 'Bob' Kilpatrick standing with Calvin, who had been practicing hockey at home in West Springfield.)

(Calvin's hockey team—the Holyoke GE "clinched the Independent Division with the win" in the Connecticut Valley Hockey League in 1949.)

“THIS DAY IN LOCAL SPORTS”

“Feb. 20, 1949: Lou Madru and Calvin Coolidge scored two goals each as Holyoke GE defeated the Ludlow Wildcats 4-1 in a Connecticut Valley Hockey League game at the Coliseum. GE clinched the Independent Division with the win.” *[This article was published in the local paper. Calvin played left wing on the championship team for three years and was leading scorer in 1948 and 1949.]*

(An example of Calvin’s sense of humor: He saw the sign, “STOP,” and stopped. Then made sure to photograph the moment.)

(This photo taken on October 8, 1950, is of Calvin's Aunt Ellen Adeline Coolidge, Franklin's sister. She was born May 26, 1906, and died in 1984. At this point in time, Ellen was living with her mother, Lillie, in her home on 11 Coolidge Drive in New Salem, Massachusetts. Her father, Harry, had passed away in 1944.)

1950

(Calvin entered the Army on September 26, 1950, and served as a 57-mm recoilless rifle squad leader with the 32nd Inf. Regt. His division played a significant role in the Korean War.)

AUGUST 1950						
S	M	T	W	T	F	S
		1	2	3	4	5
6	7	8	9	10	11	12
13	14	15	16	17	18	19
20	21	22	23	24	25	26
27	28	29	30	31		

SEPTEMBER 1950						
S	M	T	W	T	F	S
					1	2
3	4	5	6	7	8	9
10	11	12	13	14	15	16
17	18	19	20	21	22	23
24	25	26	27	28	29	30

OCTOBER 1950						
S	M	T	W	T	F	S
1	2	3	4	5	6	7
8	9	10	11	12	13	14
15	16	17	18	19	20	21
22	23	24	25	26	27	28
29	30	31				

SEPTEMBER
26
TUESDAY

Cloudy 36-6-10, 72-8-15, 82-1-15, 57-6-15

Today is the Birthday of

8:00

8:30 I done a little of my ironing

9:00

9:30 Calvin has got to go into the

10:00 service

10:30

11:00 Franklin come about 8-30

11:30 to work on wheel

12:00

12:30 Eastern States men brought the white

1:00 paint for front of house $16.28

1:30

2:00 Angie come over and gave us 2 water

2:30 melons

3:00 (I wet my flowers)

3:30

4:00 Franklin took me with him up to

4:30 Orange got a case of dog food and

5:00 a case of White House milk $9.70

5:30 and a bag of flour 2.28

6:00

6:30 Franklin went home about 6-45

7:00 I gave him part of watermelon

7:30

8:00

To reform a man, you must begin with his grandmother—Victor Hugo (96) 269

(A page from Lillie Pierce Coolidge's diary dated September 26, 1950. Lillie was Calvin's grandmother on his father Franklin's side. Diary entry third from the top reads, "Calvin has got to go into the service.")

Letters from Calvin to his Parents

September 30, 1950
Fort Devens

Dear Mom & Dad,

As I am writting this letter tonight I am expecting to be called to be sent to a training base. Today we were separated into different ranks. The fellow who is from Agawam and bunks next to me is leaving in the same outfit. *[Agawam is about three miles south of West Springfield, Massachusetts.]* We both asked for the signal Core as our first chance in what we would like to get into. This outfit trains for radar, radio & etc. This does not seem we will get what we asked for. Although we are leaving very soon they have not told us where we will go. We won't know until we get there either. You will not hear from me until I get at my next base. We don't hear much on the outside world. In fact I don't even know how the ball teams are doing. How are things in Korea!! (Ha, Ha) they don't tell us anything here. One day seems just like the other. Today is the first time the sun has shown. Until next time which will probably be at another base I will sign off

Love Cal

P.S. Do not write until you hear from me at basic because as I said in my other letter we will leave in 4 or 5 days from arrival which would mean today or tomorrow.

October 3, 1940 [1950]
[Ft. Devens]

Dear Mom & Dad,

Well here I am at my basic camp and guess where?!! Right here at Camp Devens. I am still with the fellow from Agawam Frank Carabelo. We left the reception camp late Sunday. It took us about 10 min. to get to our present camp. Same fellows are taking basic in North Carolina, Virginia, New Jersey, Ohio, Kentucky, Texas, and Washington and here I am at Ft. Devens only 80 miles away from home.

Since we arrived here we have had classes on maps.

I expect to get a weekend pass very soon. I will come home then.

I have been going to the show every night since I got here. We are off at 5:00 everyday and get up at 5:45. The food is not to [too] bad. Will be home as soon as possible.

Love Cal

P.S. How's everybody home. Is everything OK. Let me know. Write!! The address is on the envelope. Did dad get the waterwheel done.

[There is a page or two missing here...]

...reading and have had plenty of marching and drilling. The outfit I am with is a Tennessee outfit. The 278th Infantry Regiment Combat Team, Co. H 2nd Battalion. These boys were in the National Guards in Tenn. and now they are up here giving us 'basic' training. I have been told that this outfit will be ready for combat duty by Feb. 21st and will leave for Germany. This is at present just a rumor.

The squad that I am on in the regiment fires 75 mm guns. It is manned by 5 men. It weighs about 165 lbs. We are supposed to knock out machine gun nests and pill boxes...

[missing page]

[The U.S. Army reactivated Fort Devens as a class one installation in July, 1948. With the outbreak of the Korean Conflict, Fort Devens was designated as a reception center for the third time in history. No divisions were assigned to Fort Devens during the 1950s but two regimental combat teams were assigned, along with two signal battalions; the United States Army Security Agency Training Center and School; the 56th AAA Brigade; the First Army Chemical Defense School; and many smaller units.]

October 10, 1950
[Ft. Devens]

Dear Mother & Dad,

Received your letter and I was sure glad to hear from you. Since I wrote you last I have been assigned as assistant gunner on the 75 mm. This does not mean I will do this for 21 months. I was told by our Lt. that we could apply for transfer after our basic. Incidentally our basic will be over by Nov. 1st. We leave for Ft. Edwards Oct. 22 to fire our basic weapons (MI, carbine, & 45 caliber pistol) or what ever weapon we are assigned to carry. I was assigned to carry a 45 caliber pistol. As yet I have not found out what my duties will be on the 75 mm gun. After basic we are supposed to get training as a team on the 75 mm here at Fort Devens. The purpose of this gun is to blast out machine gun nests, pill boxes & tanks. (over) This weapon is new as far as the Army is concerned, having been used and experimented with since 1945. It has a range of 7200 yards.

By your letter I see you saw me in the groupe picture by the bus. You didn't see me in the other picture (swearing in) because we were sworn on in two groupes. The picture was taken of the second groupe.

We have plenty of clothes.
4 sets of sturdy clothes
2 " " winter underwear
2 sets of fatigues (work clothes)
1 class A uniform"
Combat boots
Rain coat
Field jacket

This is not all though. We will get another class A uniform, dress shoes, combat boots etc.

I haven't got a GI haircut yet. I think I will sign off for now because I have to wash some clothes (what a job). Lights out at 11:00 and morning comes only to [too] soon.

Love Cal

P.S. And wishing Dad a happy birthday. Good chance of getting a pass (no promise). Sure hope so.

November 14, 1950
[Ft. Devens]

Dear Folks,

I am just writting you a few lines to tell you that my chances of coming home Thanksgiving are very good. We will probably be off Wed. afternoon and will have to be back by Thursday midnight. Since no Tenn. boys will be able to have time to get home Thanksgiving, the Cpt. said that all boys living near the camp will be able to go home. I do not know yet if I will be home this coming weekend.

What time did "you all" (Tenn. Style) get home last Sunday night? Well it is time for 'lights out' so I will close for now.

Love Cal

P.S. If you get a chance Dad will you get my skates sharpened at the colliseum. You can get them sharpened any night there is public skating!

("Fort Devens is a United States Army Reserve military installation in the towns of Ayer and Shirley, in Middlesex County and Harvard in Worcester County in the U.S. state of Massachusetts. It was named after jurist and Civil War general Charles Devens." – Wikipedia. Calvin was located about 1 1/2 hours northeast of home in West Springfield.)

1951

(Ronald W. Bein, Aunt Mable's son. Aunt Mable "Nesbit" was Doris Coolidge's sister. Her other sister, Ruth, lived in North Carolina. Ronald was Ann and Calvin Coolidge's cousin. Ronald was in the Air Force. On March 14, 1955, Ronald Bein married Jean Elizabeth Anderson in Westfield, Massachusetts.)

[On "U. S. Air Force" letterhead]

Letter from Ronald, Calvin's cousin, to Doris and Franklin

Pvt. Ronald W. Bein - AF 11204727
3595th Basic Training Detachment
3595th Air Base Group
Nellis A.F.Base
Las Vegas, Nevada

4 Feb. 51

Dear Aunt Doris & Uncle Frank,

How are you? Fine I hope. I am doing pretty good myself. I spent a lousy month at Texas, sleeping in a tent the last week that I was there. Believe me, at night it got pretty cold down there. But that month is considered as wasted time and now I am in Las Vegas, Nevada for another five weeks of basic training.

It's really nice here though. The food is a lot better and the officers are good to us. Our basic ends March 4th and then I'm supposed to receive my P.F.C. stripes. (Private first class.) It is said that we will work on the job here for a while and then go overseas. I am trying to get into the "marines." That is an Air Force outfit that is trained to rescue pilots that crash into the ocean or lakes, and is somewhat like the navy, but my first choice is aviation mechanic, one good thing about this basic is that we have Saturday afternoons and all day Sunday to ourselfs. Yesterday I did all my washing by hand and am tired of it. Well, I'll close for now, so give my regards to Ann & Cal.

As Ever,
Ronnie

(This photo is of Nellis Air Force Base in 1956.
Photo courtesy of the Nellis Air Force Base website.)

Letters from Calvin to his Parents
Thurs. [Feb.] 22, 1951
[Postal stamp date Feb 28, 1951]

Dear Mother, Dad & Ann,

It is 9:15 PM (Thurs) Central Standard Time somewhere in Ill. I am in bed and am writting while the train has stopped because it is almost impossible to write while the train is moving. We are all riding on Pullman cars and they are very comfortable. I was lucky and am sharing a compartment with two other fellows. We have our own private bathroom.

We left Ft Devens at 4:15 PM Wed., hitting Schenectady, N.Y. in the late evening. During the night our train passed through Buffalo, New York and went through Erie, Penn. early the next morning (Thurs). We passed through Cleveland, Ohio around noon.

The scenery is rather dull looking out here this time of year. All flat and dirty looking with only a house here and there and a few small towns.

(Feb 23, 1951) Page 2

I am continuing this letter while the train has stopped here in Wichita, Kansas for a few minutes, 5:30 PM. During last night we passed through St. Louis, Missouri and stopped at Springfield early this morning. The train is not making as good time today as it did yesterday. Wichita is an up-and-coming city. We can see thousands of new homes and many more being built here. The train stops at just about all the towns. One town gave us, candy, magazines, etc.

The weather so far has been warm with springlike weather here in Kansas. The train is moving now so I will continue as soon as possible.

Well here I am in bed again (9:45 PM). The train has just stopped at the little town in Oklahoma. I just heard the conductor say we would be in Amarillo, Texas by 5:30 AM tomorrow (Sat 24, 1951) and would stop to take on supplies (linen, food, etc).

The time is 10:30 PM Pacific Time. We are either in Arizona or just over the border into California. It is to [too] dark out for me to tell. Today (Sat 24, 1951) we traveled through New Mexico and Arizona. New Mexico is not very scenic. The small towns are filled with either Indians or Mexicans. In some places the Indians still live in crude stone or mud huts.

In Arizona we started to climb and at one point we were over 8000 ft above sea level. It was snowing on and off at this elevation. Because Arizona is so far south there is very little snow on the ground. In New Mexico we stopped at Vaughn and Gallup, two small towns. In Arizona we went through Holbrook and Flagstaff.

I thought by telling you a few of the towns we passed through you might be able to trace our trip on a map. Well our train is starting to move again so I will finish the last part of this letter tomorrow when we reach our destination.

Sun 25, 1951

Arrived here at Camp Stoneman, Calf. at around 2:00 PM Pacific Time. The Camp is located in Pittsburgh, Calf. about 45 miles outside of San Francisco. The Camp is nothing but a replacement center for overseas duty. As we went up through Calif. towards camp, we passed through lush farm land. To the South and West of the camp, there are green rolling hills which sure look good as pasture and grazing land. These hills are backed by snowcapped mountains. Calif. looks like a good place to live but West Springfield sure would look a hell of a lot better about now. Except for being a little on the tired side I am feeling swell.

Well I think I will close this letter and hit the sack for a little sleep is going to field [feel] mighty good. Hope you are all well and in good health.

Lots of love to all
Cal

P.S. I'll be looking for that letter. This is the longest letter I have ever written, 3000 miles long.

Letter from Ronald to Doris

28 Feb. 51

Dear Aunt Doris,

I certainly hope that this letter finds you in the best of health. I am just getting over a bad sore throat that has bothered me for the past three days. My basic training ends this week and am I happy about it. Tomorrow I will find out just what job I will perform. Received a letter from Shirl today and was really glad to hear from her. *["Shirl" was Ann and Calvin Coolidge's cousin, and the editor's 2nd cousin. Photo below.]* She has done a lot for me, she certainly is a swell sister. Gee, it's too bad that Cal has to go to Korea. I sure hope that this war ends pretty quick. According to the papers down here, the "reds" are taking quite a beating at this time. We have been trained in the use of the M6 rifle, and I did pretty good on the shooting range, scoring as "sharpshooter." They told us that we may need that training if we are ever sent to an overseas base. Well, it's getting near bed time, so I'll close for now. Say hello to the rest of the family for me, and I will write again soon.

Love As Ever,
Ronnie

(Johnny and Shirley "Shirl" Gilbert. Shirley was Ann and Calvin's cousin.)

Letter from Calvin to his Parents

March 5, 1951

Dear Folks,

I am writting a few lines while I have a chance for we are leaving this camp sometime today. The way everything looks I guess we are headed for Japan. They have been issuing us equipment all week.

Did you get my records. Well folks I've got to cut this letter short for we have got to fall out with full equipment very shortly. Don't worry if you don't hear from me for a couple of weeks because I imagine we will be on the boat that long. I am feeling great and am in good health

Love, Cal

Letter from Ronald to Doris and Franklin

Pvt. Ronald W. Bein A.F. 11204727
Indian Springs A.F. Base
Rt. I Box 18
Indian Springs, Nevada
6 March 51

Dear Aunt Doris & Uncle Frank,

I hope that this letter finds the both of you in good health. I am fine but pretty well disgusted. I am finally out of basic and working on the job. Believe me, I would rather take four years of basic training than be where I am and doing what I am. This base is located about 50 miles out on the desert, and we are "stranded" from civilization.

The purpose of this base is to run a bombing and firing range for fighter pilots that are going to Korea. It is the only base of that sort in the country, and the world's aerial gunnery match is held here every year. We construct targets, watch the planes as they approach the targets to fire on them and tell them their faults, and score the number of hits on the targets. It may sound interesting but to me it is very boring. It wouldn't be too bad if we were closer to town. Well I guess that everyone can't have what they want in this man's Air Force, so I'll make the best of it. It is about super [supper] time now so I'll close and write again soon. Say hello to Ann for me will you?

Love, Ronnie [Bein]

("Troops assembling at Camp Stoneman for shipping out to Korea." Photo by Hanson A. Williams, Jr., Pepperdine University Libraries Digital Collections.)

Letter from Calvin to his Parents

Pvt. John C Coolidge
7th Repl. Co. 7th Inf. Div.
A.P.O. 7% Postmaster
San Francisco, Calif

March 22, 1951

Dear Folks,

I am writting you this letter on the train in Japan somewhere between Yokohama and Sasebo. The latter city is located on the island of Kyushu in the southern part of Japan.

Arrived in Yokohama late Mon. afternoon, just two weeks after leaving Camp Stoneman in Calif. The first night at sea was the roughest with just about everybody getting seasick, including myself. Most of us were only sick for a day however. The food on the ship was very good. We always had all we could eat.

I was sure glad to see land even though it was Japan. I guess everybody else felt about the same way after seeing nothing but rolling ocean for two weeks.

They had movies and church services on the boat and I went to both. The name of the boat was the General Hase. *[USS General W.F. Hase, photo and notation below.]* There were about 1700 hundred of us on board. This included Navy, Army, Air Corps, Rangers, and marine personnel. One of the movies I saw was "Dancing in the Dark" with Mark Stevens, William Powell, Adolphe Menjou, and a newcomer Betsy Drake. It was in technicolor and it played in the States about a year ago. It was about a girl who wanted to make good in the movies. And guess where she was from? Springfield, Mass. Boy did I give out a cheer!! The picture was very good.

We got off the boat Tues morning the 20th and there was a band there to greet us. In fact everywhere you go they've got bands. From the Yokohama we went to Camp Drake which is located a few miles outside of Tokyo. There we got more processing (issued clothes, checked personal affairs, etc) Left Camp Drake Thurs. morning

("USS General W. F. Hase (AP-146) was a General G. O. Squier-class transport ship for the US Navy in World War II. She was named in honor of US Army Major General William Frederick Hase. She was transferred to the US Army as USAT General W. F. Hase in 1946. On 1 March 1950 she was transferred to the Military Sea Transportation Service (MSTS) as USNS General W. F. Hase (T-AP-146). She was later sold for commercial operation in 1968, before being scrapped in 1985." *Wikipedia.*)

[Letter continued...]

(Today), the 22nd and will get in Sasebo in 36 hrs. I don't know how long we will be there. The only time we have to ourselves is when we're ridding [riding]. And we've sure had plenty of that.

The people here in Japan are very friendly. They seem to take a lot of pride in their work. They all give you a big wave when the train goes by. Even the smallest babies on their mother's back. When the train stops we throw out candy to the kids.

I received your first four letters while on the train going from the boat to Camp Drake and it sure was good to hear from all of you at home. I was surprised but glad to hear about Carol having her baby. I hope they are all doing well (including Sully). Tell him to write. I will try to write him tonight if I get a chance. Well we are in Sasebo. I will finish the letter at the camp there.

I am continuing this letter in the Service Club here at Camp Mower in Sasebo. They have issued us our orders and have told us what outfit we're in. I am in the 7th Inf. All the fellows that came from Co H at Devens are also in that outfit and we are still together here.

Today (Sat. Mar 24) we go across to Korea and land at Pusan where we will get more processing. *[In 2000, they changed the city's name to Busan.]* I know how this may all sound to you at home, but don't worry. I am in the best of health and my moral [morale] is high. I am glad to hear that the "Indians" are winning (Hockey). Hope they get into the playoffs. Incidentally, if they start a rotation system here in Korea I may be home in a few months. Say those pictures came out swell, didn't they. I always take them out and look at them every once and a while. I got a letter from Grandma and Aunt Ellen and must write them. Does Dad go up there often. That ring must be a beauty. Did Ann make those brownies'? They sound good to me. Tell her to write and tell me all about that boy friend of hers. (Ha Ha) Well I must close for now but will write every chance I get. Lots of Love to all.

"Cal"

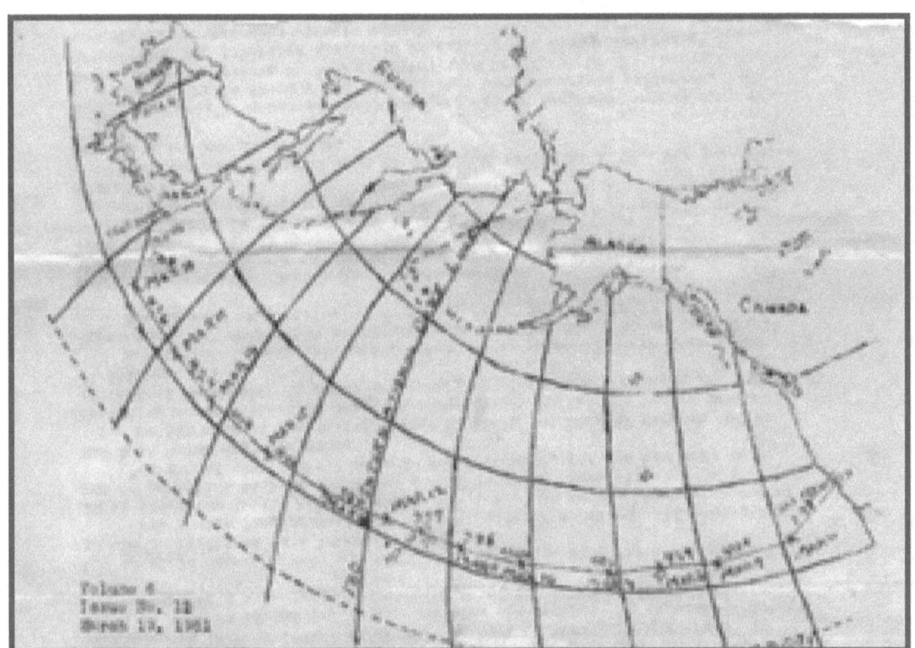

(Enclosed in the previous letter were two items. The first, above, has "Volume 6, Issue No. 12, March 19, 1951" typed in its lower left corner. Calvin might have wanted his folks to understand how the dividing line between North and South Korea came to be referred to as the 38th parallel. The 38th parallel is the circle of latitude 38 degrees north of the equator. After WWII, the USA and the USSR divided Korea in half using the actual 38th parallel line.)

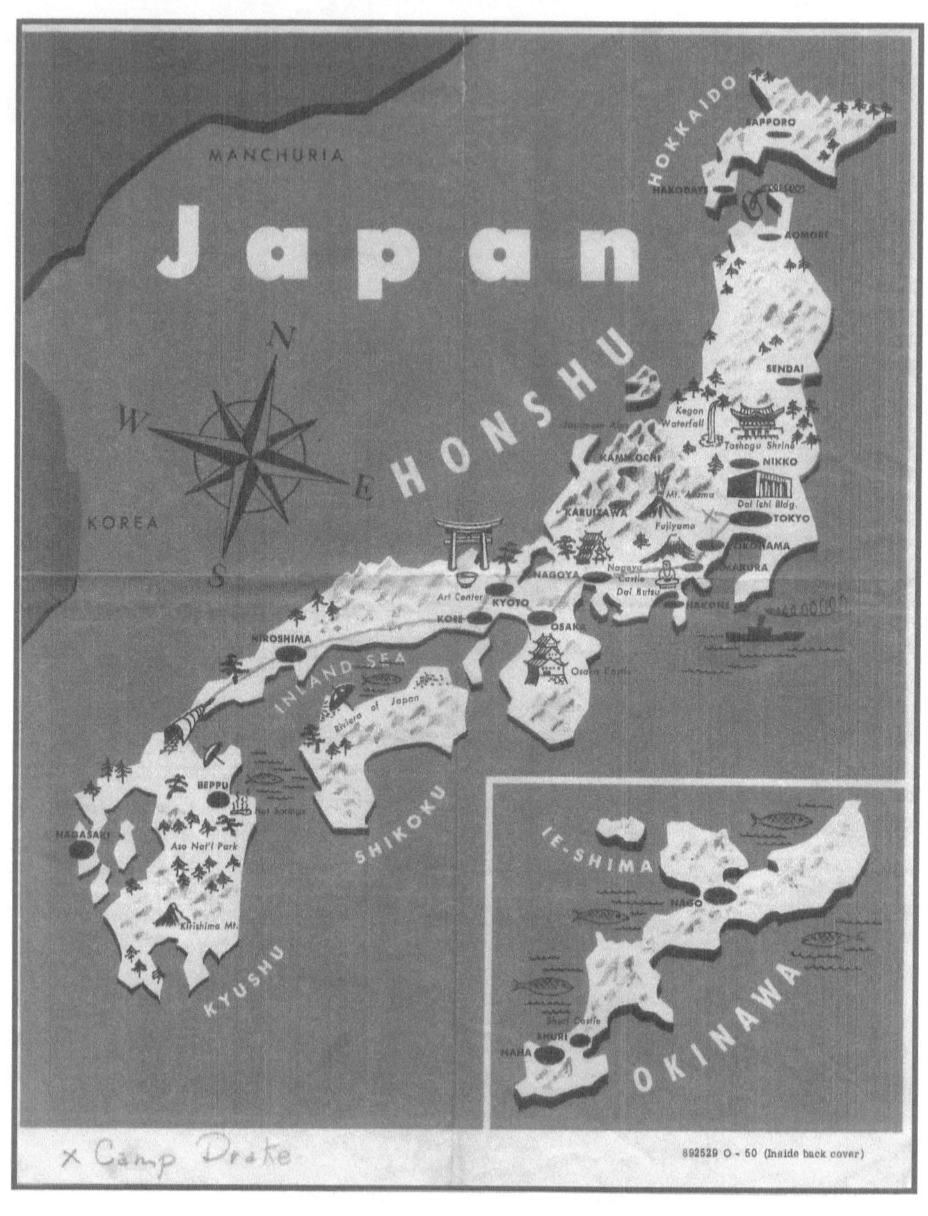

(Camp Drake is marked with an "X".
The original artifact is a bright green color.)

(Calvin Coolidge and his good friend, Richard Sullivan, or "Sully."
Photo was taken on Easter, April 21, 1946.)

[Pvt. Jerry Mason composed the following letter to his parents only seven weeks before Calvin had the same experience. Hopefully, Pvt. Mason's expressive depiction will shine more light on Calvin's trip.]

2/4/1951 Camp Mower, Sasebo, Japan

From:
Pvt. Jerry Mason
3rd INF DIV
APO-468 c/o Postmaster
S/Francisco, California

Howdy Folks,

Hows the peoples now days. Well it is in the morning on the 4th. I guess I'll be remembering this date for a long time to come. At 12:15 we load up for Korea. Say, that's a hell of a way to start out a letter isn't it. But for some reason or other that seems to bother me this morning. You know, just like owing some one a fifth of whiskey. Ha Ha. Bull shit. Well I should have written sooner but I ain't had too dam much time. Well I had time but I didn't have much to say. Is that a good enough excuse. I guess I am lazy. I ain't had time to look up Jerry and where I should start is quite a problem. For all I know he might be in Europe. I ask mom for his address so when she asks would you give it to her. And after I march through Moscow I'll find time to drop down in Austria and see Earl. Big ideas you know. I still say bull shit.

Say did you ever take a ocean cruse with all expenses paid. Dam that's nice. Well it wasn't bad after the first 6 or 7 days. Got kind of exciting at first. Up and down all the time. Piss me off. I go so mad at time I felt like jumping up and down to see if I could rock the ship more. But I didn't feel that mean all the time. It was a big basterd call the "Anderson," It carried around 3000 people all together. Crew, wacs, nurses, Army, National Guard. Quite a mess. Dam, most of the guys are getting ready to go over there.

Piss on it. I still have hope it will be over by the time I get there (36 hours). I got lots of time. Breakfast on a ocean cruse. Best you ever saw. Burnt beans, catsup and corn bread. Or stew. Or unpealed and a well burnt potatoes with a jucy apple. Oh boy, makes my mouth water. But over here the chow is realey the very best. I say it is realey good cause you get a lot and we get lots of chicken and stough like that. I saw some nice scenry on the way over here too. All kinds of it. Water, Water & we sometimes caught an occasional glimps of water. Man that's a big ocean. We took off from Frisco and came up to Seattle then dow the coast again and across by the Islands then up to Yokohama. Then we ended up in Camp Drake 14 miles north of Tokyo. I stayed there 2 ½ days and then moved down the coast by train to an island upon which this place rests. It is called Camp Mower. I'll have been here almost a day by noon when we take off. I spent 3 ½ days in Camp Stoneman (stateside) and 18 days on an ocean cruse. I guess that takes in a pretty fast trip.

These Japs are kind of in a bad way. Industry is very small. Timber is only on hills and looks like they only grow small trees. The only animals are cows and a few dogs. They must have ate the rest. Autos are few and far between. So I see why they only have a few roads and only room for one car on them. They farm every possible inch of ground. And I ain't shitting. Every dam inch. Miles of rice paddies. We got a lot of them working for the Army. K.P. and pulling all the details. They work for as little as 50 Cents a month up to almost $6 a month. Say, they are in the money. They are though realey. I guess the average guy makes about 100 yen a month. That makes that 50 cents of our money is worth 150 yen. 360 yen to $1. When we throw them a cigarette they fight like a mad pack of dogs after a bone. The train we were on must have thrown out 100 boxes of candy and 200 cartons of cigarettes. I felt like getting out and picking up a few myself. They are a dark cream colored, short average around 5 foot tall and are heavy set. They wear heavy cloths for warmth. Except for the G.I. Joes girl. They have American cloths. The guys get them from the states for their girls.

I saw a lot of scenery over here on the train. The land is an ancient looking place. Maybe it is cause of the houses and the mountains. But it is a pretty place if you don't try to notice the small things like a man taking a piss on the tracks and waveing at you at the same time. You know, small details. Or the way they build their homes and how much trash gathers around them. Trash means shit, (human) straw or anything that is fertilizer. Makes a fragerent oder. There is more to say but time has run out on me. So all you guys be good and if you can drop around and see me, I'll show you the fundamentals of Hearts. So long.

Love to all

Jerry

Letters from Calvin to his Parents

March 27, 1951

Dear Folks,

Well here I am in Korea and it's everything they said it was. Hills, hills, and more hills. The town we are in is Chechon [South Korea]. It's just like all the rest of the towns except that it has a different name and that maybe there's a few more buildings left standing. At present we are living in tents, with about 23 to a tent. We sleep in sleeping bags so it isn't to bad. It isn't cold here but gets chilly at night. There is some snow left on the higher mts. We arrived at Pusan Easter Sunday [March 25] but didn't stay long. From Pusan we went by train to our present camp, arriving about two o'clock Mon. March 26th. They are separating us into different outfits. I am in the 32nd Inf Reg. as a heavy weapons man. We will leave here tomorrow for five days of training before being assigned to a company. Just where I don't know. Patrick Connolly who is from Holyoke and was at Camp Stevens with me, is in an artillery outfit that is in direct support of the 32nd. I guess that is all I have to say at this time except that I sure will be glad when they start that rotations system they are talking about. Six months up front and then be sent back to Japan or U.S. to finish out the rest of your time. There are rumors that it may start April 1st. Even though my letters may be short, I write when ever I get a chance. I will probably have more time when I finally get assigned to a company. I haven't received a letter from you since I was in Camp Drake but we are on the move so much that I imagine it will take time for them to catch up. Because we are on the move it probably takes my letters a little time to get to you folks at home. So don't worry if you don't hear from me from time to time. There goes the chow call so I will close for now.

With lots of love to all of you.

'Cal'

P.S. If you ever have an emergency and you think you need me at home, get in touch with the local Red Cross and they will take care of the rest. They can get in touch with me a lot quicker than you can at home by writting.

April , 1951
[He includes no date on the letter.
Envelope postmarked April 14, 1951]

Dear Folks,

I am writting you while I have a few moments. Have just finished noon chow. We had turkey with all the trimmings. Incidently the meals have been extra good here in Korea, surprising as it may seem. You get all you can eat. I had two helpings. Get hungry out here in the open air.

Well I am finally assigned to a Company. (Co. K 32nd Inf.) I am in a heavy weapons platoon and am in a 57 mm recoilless rifle squad. They are the same as a 75mm only smaller. [*A recoilless rifle is a lightweight artillery system or man-portable launcher that is designed to eject some form of countermass such as propellant gas from the rear of the weapon at the moment of firing, creating forward thrust that counteracts most of the weapon's recoil. Photo below.*]

Since I wrote last in Chechon I have traveled up the East coast some 30 miles south of the 38th for a few days of training (firing weapons & watching demonstrations). From there the Co. has moved to the central sector where I am now located.

Seven other fellows that were in Co. H at Ft. Devens with me were also assigned with Co K. Three of them are with me in the heavy weapons platoon. Two of them are in the same section with me. I have pitched a pup tent with Walter Donahue. He was at Devens in Co. H.

Well how are things at home. Good I hope. Say did you hear or read about the rotation plan they are going to start over here? There is a good chance that I may be out of here in four to six months depending upon how soon they start the rotation plan. I haven't received any mail since I was at Camp Drake in Japan.

If you write to this new address however I will get mail in 10 days. I will be looking for them. Give the address to anyone that wants to write and I will answer when I get a chance. There is not much to talk about out here but will answer the letters as best I can. Does Sully have my address. I wrote him from Sasebo. Give him this address if any of you get a chance. It cost quite a lot to send packages out here but I will accept one once and a while (Ha Ha) Well until I hear from you all

Lots of Love
Cal

Pvt John C. Coolidge
US51095649 Co. K 32 Inf
APO 7 % Postmaster
San Francisco

("Korean War photos of 1951—A 57-mm recoilless rifle team opens fire at a Chinese position three miles south of the 38th Parallel in Korea. 31 March 1951. Korea. Signal Corps Photo #FEC-51-10111 (Chang)" This is the same type of recoilless rifle Calvin was trained in using and operated in Korea.)

(While Calvin was fighting overseas, his family was in church praying for him. This Easter service, dated March 25, 1951, meant so much to them that they kept the bulletin all those years, a total of 3 pages.)

ORDER OF WORSHIP March 25, 1951

EASTER SUNDAY

ORGAN-PIANO DUET Hallelujah Chorus Handel

THE EASTER ANNOUNCEMENT Choir

CONGREGATIONAL INVOCATION
Almighty God, Father of our Lord Jesus Christ, who didst raise up thy Son from the dead and give him glory, that our faith and hope might be in thee; quicken us also, we beseech thee, by thy mighty power, from the death of sin to the life of righteousness, and cause us to set our affections on things above. Amen.

HYMN 238 The Strife Is O'er

RESPONSIVE READING 15 Easter

ANTHEM A Joyous Easter Hymn

PRAYER in unison (opposite page)

SPECIAL EASTER OFFERING for Home Missions

OFFERTORY ANTHEM The Magdalene

DOXOLOGY and PRESENTATION

THE SCRIPTURE LESSON II Corinthians 4, 5:1

HYMN 240 Come, Ye Faithful, Raise the Strain

SERMON From Death to Life

HYMN 245 I Know That My Redeemer Lives

BENEDICTION (Congregation seated)

EASTER PRAYER

Eternal God, our Father, Thou hast set eternity in our hearts. We give thee thanks for the victory of our Lord Jesus Christ over death and the grave. Grant us the power of his resurection so that we may rise with Him into newness of life. Amid the deepening shadows that darken our horizon, open our eyes that we may see Him clearly as the only Light of the world. In the dark days ahead may the Way which He personified be our way. May the Truth which He revealed abide in us and be the pattern of our lives so that we may also say that not we live but Christ liveth in us. Grant us the daily experience of his abiding, living presence so that in trustful companionship with Him we may face the storms of life unafraid.

Give courage and strength to Thy church to proclaim the gospel of reconciliation among the nations that are torn asunder by bloody strife and lead them into the way of peace and good will. Enlarge in us the faith that looks with steadfast hope and confidence to the day when every knee shall bow and every tongue shall confess that Jesus Christ is Lord.

In his name we pray.

Amen

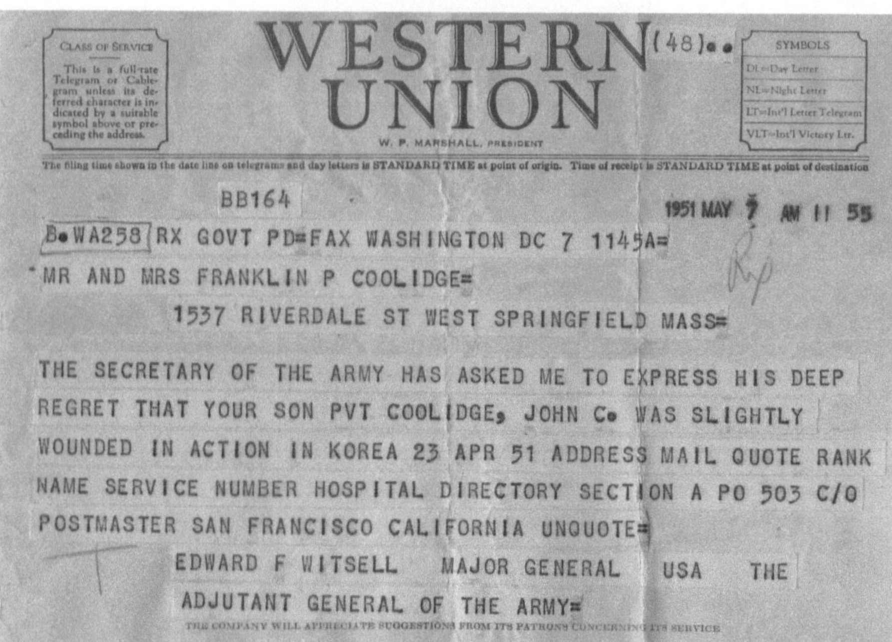

WESTERN UNION (48)..

CLASS OF SERVICE
This is a full-rate Telegram or Cablegram unless its deferred character is indicated by a suitable symbol above or preceding the address.

W. P. MARSHALL, PRESIDENT

SYMBOLS
DL=Day Letter
NL=Night Letter
LT=Int'l Letter Telegram
VLT=Int'l Victory Ltr.

The filing time shown in the date line on telegrams and day letters is STANDARD TIME at point of origin. Time of receipt is STANDARD TIME at point of destination

BB164

1951 MAY 7 AM 11 55

B.WA258 RX GOVT PD=FAX WASHINGTON DC 7 1145A=

MR AND MRS FRANKLIN P COOLIDGE=
1537 RIVERDALE ST WEST SPRINGFIELD MASS=

THE SECRETARY OF THE ARMY HAS ASKED ME TO EXPRESS HIS DEEP REGRET THAT YOUR SON PVT COOLIDGE, JOHN C. WAS SLIGHTLY WOUNDED IN ACTION IN KOREA 23 APR 51 ADDRESS MAIL QUOTE RANK NAME SERVICE NUMBER HOSPITAL DIRECTORY SECTION A PO 503 C/O POSTMASTER SAN FRANCISCO CALIFORNIA UNQUOTE=

EDWARD F WITSELL MAJOR GENERAL USA THE ADJUTANT GENERAL OF THE ARMY=

THE COMPANY WILL APPRECIATE SUGGESTIONS FROM ITS PATRONS CONCERNING ITS SERVICE

Telegram
May 7, 1951

Mr and Mrs Franklin P Coolidge
1537 Riverdale St West Springfield Mass

The Secretary of the Army has asked me to express his deep regret that your son Pvt Coolidge, John C. was slightly wounded in action in Korea 23 Apr 51 Address mail quote rank name service number hospital directory section A PO 503 c/o postmaster San Francisco California unquote=

Edward F Witsell Major General USA
The Adjutant General of the Army

WESTERN UNION
TELEGRAM

B• WA258

MR AND MRS FRANKLIN P COOLIDGE
1537 RIVERDALE ST WEST SPRINGFIEL

[The editor asked Ann Coolidge about the moment the doorbell rang and this telegram was delivered to the house. She replied, "I was working night duty as a Registered Nurse, so I slept late in the morning. When the telegram arrived, I was upstairs sleeping. My mother worked at Farmer Browns, putting together what they call 'Soup Bunches.' She wore rubber boots and stood on wet concrete all day long. So, when the telegram arrived, I was the one to answer the door. I was in my robe and went to the door. I was relieved and so happy that Cal was alive, safe, and well taken care of. He was sent to Japan to the hospital there."]

Pvt John C Coolidge
US51095649 Co. K 32nd Inf
APO 7 c/o Postmaster
San Francisco

April 26, 1951

Dear Folks,

As I write this letter from Pusan on a Danish hospital ship I suppose you have received a telegram stating I was injured in action. I was winged in the shoulder at the base of the neck. It is not serious. No broken bones so I don't get to the states yet. They treat you great here and give you the best of care. Don't want you to worry at home because I am doing great. Good chance here to rest up a bit. The food is swell. Had steak and ice cream for dinner. How does that sound? I got hit the 23rd. Some birthday present Hah. (over)

Just heard over the radio that they are going to start sending home 20,000 a month from here in May. Sounds good. Will be home before you know it. Am listening to the Kirt *[Curt]* Massey and Martha Tilton program. Reminds me of supper time at home. They come on at 5:45 Right! I am closing for now to eat chow but will write more soon. Lots of love to all.

Cal

(The Curt Massey and Martha Tilton program was sponsored by Alka-Seltzer, and began in 1949 as Curt Massey Time with Martha Tilton. The show was announced by Ford Pearson.)

(When the Danish government learned that the United Nations' effort in Korea needed help, they turned a passenger ship into a floating hospital and docked it in the Pusan Harbor. Calvin was taken on board the Jutlandia "after getting winged in the left shoulder" (letter dated April 27, 1951) during the Battle of King's Hill on Hill 902, April 23, 1951. Professors, doctors, specialists, nurses, and assistants made up the staff of 91. They would line up to welcome folks as they entered the ship docked in the Pusan Harbor. During its service in Korea, the Danish hospital treated 4,981 patients, most of whom were severely wounded, like Calvin. This photo was taken on June 27, 1950.)

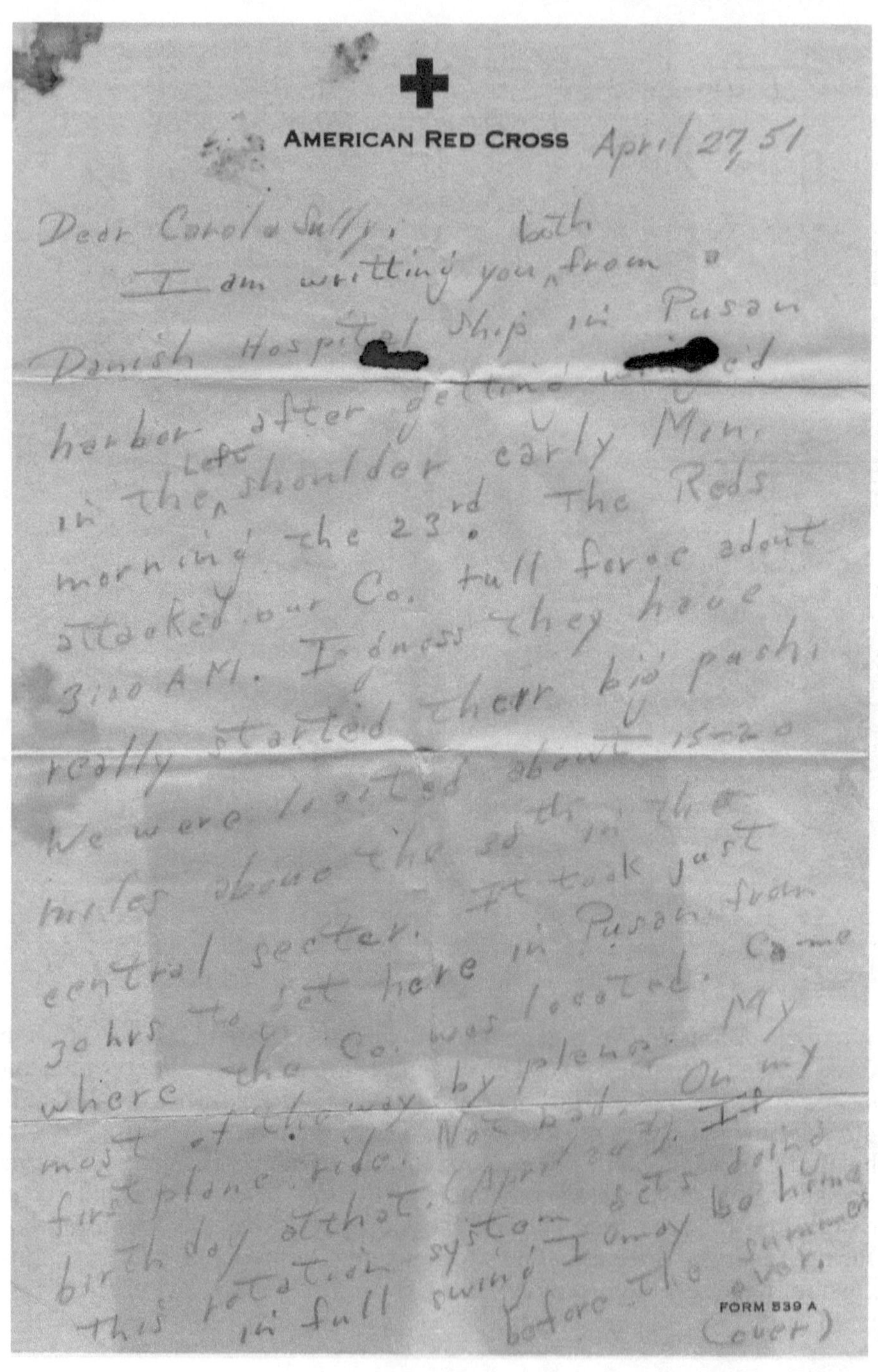

AMERICAN RED CROSS April 27, 51

Dear Carol & Sally, both

I am writting you from a Danish Hospital Ship in Pusan harbor after getting wounded in the left shoulder early Mon. morning the 23rd. The Reds attacked our Co. full force about 3:00 A.M. I guess they have really started their big push. We were located about 15 to 20 miles above the 38th in the central sector. It took just 30 hrs to get here in Pusan from where the Co. was located. Came most of the way by plane. My first plane ride. Not bad. On my birthday at that. (April 24th.) If this rotation system gets going in full swing I may be home before the summer over.

FORM 539 A

(over)

(Note the dried blood smudges in the upper left corner. In the original letter those marks are still red. Typed version of this letter follows.)

I am still anxious to hear
from you brother. How's the
little girl doing? I see by
the Stars & Stripes (A GI paper
here Korea) that the Giants [illegible] start, I am
are off [illegible]
still for them win or lose, still
Maybe they could use Big 'Jawn'
Mize Ha! Ha!
Am closing now to watch
the movies

Love
Cal

P.S. Write as often as you can
This article is about the ship
I am on. Give it to the folks
if you get a chance. thanks

Letter from Calvin to Carol and Sully

April 27, 1951 [Friday]
[Calvin was shot on Monday, April 23rd,
one day before his birthday.]

Dear Carol & Sully,

I am writting you both from Danish hospital ship in Pusan Harbor after getting winged in the left shoulder early Monday morning, the 23rd. The Reds attacked our Co. full force about 3:00 am. I guess they have really started their big push. We were located about 15 to 20 miles above the 38th in the central sector. *[The Korean war began with North Korean forces crossing the 38th parallel into South Korea on June 25, 1950.]* It took just 30 hours to get here in Pusan from where the Co. was located. Came most of the way by plane. My first plane ride. Not bad. On my birthday, at that. [April 24th]. If this rotation system gets going in full swing I may be home before the summer's over.

I am still anxious to hear from you both. How is the little girl doing? I see by the Stars and Stripes (A GI paper here in Korea) that the Giants are off to a good start. I am still for them win or lose. Maybe they could still use Big 'Jawn' Mize Ha! Ha! Am closing now to watch the movies.

Love, Cal

P.S. Write as often as you can. This article is about the ship I am on. Give it to the folks if you get a chance. Thanks.

Admiral Joy Tours Dane Hospital Ship

PUSAN (AP)—Vice Adm. C. Turner Joy, commander of U.S. Naval Forces in the Far East, Tuesday made a tour of the Danish Red Cross floating hospital Jutlandia in Pusan harbor.

The admiral had lunch aboard the vessel with her commander, Kai Hammerich.

The Jutlandia, in the first six weeks of operations in Korean waters, processed more than 800 patients and more than 400 major and minor operations have been performed on UN combat men.

World famous brain surgeon Dr. Eduard Busch, is among the four prominent Danish physicians on duty with the hospital ship.

(This is Richard Sullivan, Calvin's best friend nicknamed "Sully.")

(Military vehicles at the 38th Parallel in Korea.)

Newspaper Article
April 29, 1951
Springfield, Mass

THE SPRINGFIELD SUNDAY REPUBLICAN

One in City, Other in Korea

West Springfield, April 25—Miss Ann N. Coolidge, 22, daughter of Mr. and Mrs. Franklin P. Coolidge of 1537 Riverdale St., who graduated from New England Baptist Hospital School of Nursing, Boston, in January, will attend the formal graduation exercises at Newton Center Baptist Church, Newton, May 4. A member of the 1947 graduating class of West Springfield High School, she is now engaged in private duty nursing in Springfield. Her brother, Pvt. John Calvin Coolidge, 25, was graduated from West Springfield High School in 1943 and is now in the central sector in Korea. He entered service September, 1951. After high school he attended Stockbridge School of Agriculture and he worked at the General Electric plant in Holyoke prior to entering service. He played left wing on the championship team for three years in the Connecticut Valley Hockey League and was leading scorer in 1948 and 1949.

THE SPRINGFIELD SUNDAY REPUBLICA

One in City, Other in Korea

ANN N. COOLIDGE

PVT. JOHN C. COOLIDGE

West Springfield, April 28—Miss Ann N. Coolidge, 22, daughter of Mr. and Mrs. Franklin P. Coolidge of 1537 Riverdale St., who graduated from New England Baptist Hospital School of Nursing, Boston, in January, will attend the formal graduation exercises at Newton Center Baptist Church, Newton, May 4. A member of the 1947 graduating class of West Springfield High School, she is now engaged in private duty nursing in Springfield.

Her brother, Pvt. John Calvin Coolidge, 25, was graduated from West Springfield High School in 1943 and is now in the central sector in Korea. He entered service September, 1950. After high school he attended Stockbridge School of Agriculture and he worked at the General Electric plant in Holyoke prior to entering service. He played left wing on the championship team for three years in the Connecticut Valley Hockey League and was leading scorer in 1948 and 1949.

(Newspaper article dated April 29, 1951.)

Pvt. John Calvin Coolidge US51095649
United States Air Force Hospital
Nagoya Air Base
APO 1054 c/o PM
San Francisco, Calif.

April 30, 1951

Dear Folks,

Well, it seems that every time I write to you at home I am in a different place. This time I am back in Japan in the city of Nagoya. I am in an Army Air Corp Hospital. It is a swell hospital as hospitals go.

My shoulder is coming along fine. The doctor told me today that I would be here from 4 - 6 weeks. That's OK by me. They have a PX here at the hospital and a snack bar also. The meals are the best I have seen since I have been in the Army. I have been eating most of the time since I got here. They have movies every other day and the Red Cross has a recreation room with ping pong and pool tables. They also have a lounge (reading, music, etc).

I left the Danish Hospital ship yesterday morning and flew by plane to Nagoya. It took nearly three hrs. The plane was a C54. You know I haven't received a letter since I was at Camp Drake over a month ago. I guess I just haven't been in one place long enough. I ought to get mail here however. I sure hope so. Will write again Tomorrow.

Love, 'Cal'

Pvt John C Coolidge USST095649
United States Air Force Hosp.
Nagoya Air Base
APO 1054 % Postmaster
San Francisco, Calif.

May 1, 1951

Dear Folks,

I am still enjoying my stay here. Plenty of magazines and books to read. Plenty of good food to eat. Red Cross holds movies or stage shows every night. What more could a guy ask for except to get home.

I think they made a mistake in relieving MacArthur of his Command here. *[Douglas MacArthur led the United Nations Command in the Korean War.]* Don't you. Sounds like more politics. Dean Acheson I think should be relieved. He is no statesman.

How's Ann doing at nursing? Could use a good nurse here. How's Dale? How are the people down stairs. Are you going to have a garden? Do Shirley & Johnney come over often? That's all I can do is ask questions until I here from you. (over)

Is the Ford still running. Have made apointments with the dentist while I am here in the hospital. It looks like I'll get my teeth fixed up anyway.

Not much news so will close for now. Lots of Love to ALL

'Cal'

May 5, 1951

Dear Folks,

Writting a few lines to let you know that I am feeling great. Doc looked at my shoulder today and said it looked good. Will sew it up sometime next week probably.

I've been eating so much and so often that I weigh 160 lbs. The most I have ever weighed.

I was reading the "Stars & Stripes" when I came across this article which I think you may be interested in reading. It tells all about the Co. I am in (King Co.). That was the morning I got hit in the shoulder. That's the way the UN line was hit at different places along the whole front that morning. If they don't start using some of MacArthur's ideas over here we are going to get nowhere. Just the way we are now.

How's everything back home. Good I hope. Not working to hard? Good!! Will close for now (noon chow, don't want to miss it. Ha Ha!! I am getting fat)

Lots of Love
To All
'Cal'

[Enclosed with this letter was the following article in "Stars & Stripes" Volume 7, Number 124, Friday, May 4, 1951.]

(Company K, 32D Regimental Combat Team, Nearing The Top Of Another Hill. Smoke is from white phosphorus shells.)

Bitter Battle Of 'Kings Hill' Will Long Be Remembered By 32d

WITH 7TH DIV (Pac. S&S)— There's a hill in Korea that will long be remembered by the 32d "Queen's Own" Regiment.

It's called "Hill 902" on the map. But, in the minds of fighting men, it will be remembered as "King's Hill." It was there that King company fought one of its bitterest battles.

King company, commanded by 1st Lt. Joseph P. Kingston, Yakima, Wash., occupied the ridge line on the west of Hill 902. Item company, commanded by Capt. Byron Meadows, held hill positions north of the ridge.

They expected the banzai attack.

AT MIDNIGHT it began. The first few elements of the Communist force charged Item company at five minutes after midnight. From then on it was a four-hour melee. The North Koreans charged wildly, blindly, throwing grenades as they swarmed over the company's positions. Still they held.

Finally, when the hill was covered with living and dead Communists, Captain Meadows rallied his company and drew back to King company's left flank. King came under the attack in the pale light of dawn.

The frenzied North Koreans charged up the hill in droves, dodging around rocks up the steep slope, screaming and yelling. Red after Red fell, but still they came. The Communists drove in close to throw hand grenades and the fighting grew to hand to hand combat. There were fixed bayonets.

THE RAGING Reds managed to drive a wedge into King company's positions late that morning. There were North Koreans on all sides of the hill. The brave GIs held to their guns. They were holding to two small islands in a sea of maniacal Reds.

Then the GIs launched an attack of their own, charging from the right and left. Their line along the ridge was restored. They slashed at the Reds below them on all sides. Enemy dead continued to pile up.

About the middle of the afternoon the attack was considered contained but there were still Communists at the bottom of the hill.

The following night Able company, under command of Capt. Ted Wallace, Columbia, S. C., moved back from the right flank to take over King company's position's. King shifted to the left while Item dropped back into reserve.

THE MEN of King company dropped into their foxholes. They were stunned, dazed and tired but they had to dig in and hold their positions during the long night. The main force of the attack had been either killed or driven back. But a few die-hard Reds holed up. The GIs were at their guns in the morning, taking turns blasting at the Reds who showed their heads, while buddies caught a few moments sleep during the day.

Word came to Able Company's CP at noon that an enemy force was sighted moving toward their positions. They were ordered to send a platoon to the front and head off the Reds.

"THEY MUST have thought we were going to banzai them." Captain Wallace said when the platoon came back. "But, hell, they had enough people down there to eat up everybody here."

An air strike on a hill to the front brought the fleeing Reds out into the open roads and fields. Able and King company's machineguns opened up on them. It was a turkey shoot.

Everyone knew at the sight of the Reds fleeing in the distance that the defense of King's Hill was accomplished. It was a case of heroism—united heroism. No one man was more of a hero than the other.

(Newspaper clipping from Friday, May 4, 1951. Stars and Stripes, Pacific, Volume 7, Number 124. Calvin was in the 32nd division. Typed version follows.)

Newspaper Article
Friday, May 4, 1951
Stars (Pacific) And Stripes
Volume 7, Number 124

BITTER BATTLE OF "KINGS HILL' WILL LONG BE REMEMBERED BY 32D

With 7th Div (Pac. S&S) –

There's a hill in Korea that will long be remembered by the 32d "Queen's Own" Regiment.

It's called "Hill 902" on the map. But, in the minds of fighting men, it will be remembered as "King's Hill." It was there that King company fought one of its bitterest battles.

King company, commanded by 1st Lt. Joseph P. Kingston, Yakima, Wash., occupied the ridge line on the west of Hill 902. Item company, commanded by Capt. Byron Meadows, held hill positions north of the ridge.

They expected the banzai attack.

At midnight it began. The first few elements of the Communist force charged Item company at five minutes after midnight. From then on it was a four-hour melee. The North Koreans charged wildly, blindly, throwing grenades as they swarmed over the company's positions. Still they held.

Finally, when the hill was covered with living and dead Communists, Captain Meadows rallied his company and drew back to King company's left flank. King came under the attack in the pale light of dawn.

The frenzied North Koreans charged up the hill in droves, dodging around rocks up the steep slope, screaming and yelling. Red after Red fell, but still they came. The Communists drove in close to throw hand grenades and the fighting grew to hand to hand combat. There were fixed bayonets.

THE RAGING Reds managed to drive a wedge into King company's positions late that morning. There were North Koreans on all sides of the hill. The brave GIs held to their guns. They were holding to two small islands in a sea of maniacal Reds.

Then the GIs launched an attack of their own, charging from the right and left. Their line along the ridge was restored. They slashed at the Reds below them on all sides. Enemy dead continued to pile up.

About the middle of the afternoon the attack was considered contained but there were still Communists at the bottom of the hill.

The following night Able company, under command of Capt. Ted Wallace, Columbia, S. C., moved back from the right flank to take over King company's position's [positions]. King shifted to the left while Item dropped back into reserve.

THE MEN of King company dropped into their foxholes. They were stunned, dazed and tired but they had to dig in and hold their positions during the long night. The main force of the attack had been either killed or driven back. But a few die-hard Reds holed up. The GIs were at their guns in the morning, taking turns blasting at the Reds who showed their heads, while buddies caught a few moments of sleep during the day.

Word came to Able Company's CP at noon that an enemy force was sighted moving toward their positions. They were ordered to send a platoon to the front and head off the Reds.

"THEY MUST have thought we were going to banzai them." Captain Wallace said when the platoon came back. "But, hell, they had enough people down there to eat up everybody here."

An air strike on a hill to the front brought the fleeing Reds out into the open roads and fields. Able and King company's machineguns opened up on them. It was a turkey shoot.

Everyone knew at the sight of the Reds fleeing in the distance that the defense of King's Hill was accomplished. It was a case of heroism —united heroism. No one man was more of a hero than the other.

(Calvin's Purple Heart.)

(Ann graduated from the New England Baptist Hospital School of Nursing in Boston in January 1951. She then attended the formal graduation exercises at Newton Center Baptist Church on May 4, 1951, the same day that the article on Calvin's division, King Company's "Bitter Battle," was published.)

COMMENCEMENT WEEK

New England Baptist Hospital
School of Nursing

May First to Sixth
Nineteen Hundred Fifty-one

(The program for Ann Coolidge's commencement, 5 pages total.)

Calendar for Commencement Week

Tuesday, May First
ALUMNAE ENTERTAINING
THE GRADUATING CLASS
at the "Pops"

Thursday, May Third
HOSPITAL ENTERTAINING
THE GRADUATING CLASS
Banquet
Six-forty-five o'clock

INTERMEDIATE CLASS ENTERTAINING
THE GRADUATING CLASS
Theatre Party
Eight-thirty o'clock

Friday, May Fourth
THE EVENING OF GRADUATION
Newton Centre Baptist Church
Newton Centre, Massachusetts
Eight-fifteen o'clock

Saturday, May Fifth
RECEPTION OF THE JUNIOR CLASS
TO THE GRADUATING CLASS
Longwood Towers, Brookline
Nine o'clock

Sunday, May Sixth
FLORENCE NIGHTINGALE SERVICE
MASSACHUSETTS STATE COUNCIL OF STUDENT NURSES
John Hancock Hall
Eight o'clock

The Evening of Graduation

Program

MR. CLARENCE E. ALLEN, *Presiding*
Chairman, School of Nursing Committee

PRELUDE — Mr. Gerald F. Frazee, *Organist*

PROCESSIONAL: March Pontificale — *Gounod*

AMERICA (last stanza) — School and Audience

INVOCATION — The Rev. Everett C. Herrick, D.D.

GREETINGS — Mr. Clarence E. Allen

SONGS

Service — *Charles Wakefield Cadman*

Lift Thine Eyes
from "Elijah" — *Felix Mendelssohn*

Where E'er You Walk — *George Friedrich Handel*

Mr. Gerald F. Frazee, *Organ*
Mr. Donald L. Marshall, *Conducting*

ADDRESS — The Rev. Russell H. Bishop
Pastor, Newton Centre Baptist Church

PRESENTATION OF DIPLOMAS — Mr. Bradford C. Patch, *President*

PRESENTATION OF AWARDS — Dr. Albert A. Hornor
Member, School of Nursing Committee

HYMN 371 — School and Audience

BENEDICTION — The Rev. Everett C. Herrick, D.D.

RECESSIONAL

March of the Priests, from "Athalia" — *Mendelssohn*

Reception

Members of Graduating Class

*Coolidge, Ann Nesbit	West Springfield, Massachusetts
*Ellis, Priscilla Collingwood	Plymouth, Massachusetts
*Harvey, Emma Ida	Leominster, Massachusetts
*Hasty, Dorothy Estelle	Cape Elizabeth, Maine
*Hoar, Joanne	Millis, Massachusetts
*Landers, Lois Ann	Lynn, Massachusetts
*Moses, Cynthia Anne	Bath, Maine
*Langelier, Irene Rose	Rochester, New Hampshire
*McCoy, Barbara Anne	Fall River, Massachusetts
*Pickard, Nancy Estelle	Chelmsford, Massachusetts
*Young, Marie Helen	North Pembroke, Massachusetts
Backman, Elizabeth Arden	Ellsworth, Maine
Bergeron, Joan Victoria	Fall River, Massachusetts
Black, Rose Margaret	Barre, Vermont
Brackett, Judith Isabelle	Eastham, Massachusetts
Burbank, Marie	Needham, Massachusetts
Campbell, Ruth Eleanor	Quincy, Massachusetts
Carter, Barbara Elkins	Bowdonham, Maine
Cate, Virginia Emma	Concord, New Hampshire
Clark, Winifred Evelyn	North Westport, Massachusetts
Crane, Shirley Elizabeth	DeLand, Florida
Cummings, Mrs. Barbara Ann Siegars	Newtonville, Massachusetts
Cummings, Selma Rae	Bath, Maine
Currier, Priscilla Ann	Laconia, New Hampshire
Currier, Thelma Ann	West Springfield, Massachusetts
Davis, Mildred Jeanne	Kennebunk Port, Maine
Edie, Carol Edna	Greenwich, New York
Frey, Mary Elizabeth	Vineyard Haven, Massachusetts
Galloway, Nancy Ann	Methuen, Massachusetts
Gardner, Pauline Louise	Bartlett, New Hampshire
Gibbs, Ann	Marion, Massachusetts
Hall, Joan Mary	Kennebunk, Maine
Hastings, Norma Mae	North Springfield, Vermont
Heal, Ada May	Hampton Falls, New Hampshire
Hersom, Geraldine June	Rochester, New Hampshire
Kallstrom, Betty Marie	Worcester, Massachusetts
Litchfield, Frances Elizabeth	Ellsworth, Maine
Lovett, Ruth Flora	Bangor, Maine
McLean, Ruth Ann	Ludlow, Massachusetts
Mullen, Annie Louise	Blaine, Maine

Noyes, Barbara Ann	Newburyport, Massachusetts
Noyes, Leslie	Spencer, Massachusetts
Papoojian, Dorothy Ann	Haverhill, Massachusetts
Rafter, Betty Ellen	West Medway, Massachusetts
Ray, Leta Jane	West Springfield, Massachusetts
Sample, Norma Wiley	Brookline, Massachusetts
Stein, Elizabeth	North Weymouth, Massachusetts
Tower, Arlene Viola	Caryville, Massachusetts
Tryon, Phyllis Arleen	Pownal, Maine
Wallace, Beatrice Olga	Antrim, New Hampshire
Waterhouse, Martha Joan	Bethel, Maine
Whelpley, Lois Marguerite	Milton, Massachusetts
Wood, Betsy Meeker	Morristown, New Jersey
Woodland, Jean Burton	Westport, Massachusetts
†Crooks, Norma Virginia	Brookfield, Massachusetts
†Hauer, Beverly Anne *	Hartford, Connecticut
†Hultgren, Phyllis Lindette	Meriden, Connecticut
†Mikell, Mary Thurston	Staatsburg, New York
†Thompson, Ann Loretta	Houlton, Maine
†Young, Mrs. Natalie Ann Conner	Auburn, Maine

* Course Completed

† Bates College 5-Year Program

The Audience will kindly not applaud until the last diploma has been presented.

Letter from Calvin to Sully

May 6, 1951

Dear Sully,

How's the old family man doing? Incidently keep building that family until you are sure Uncle Sam doesn't want or can get your services. Anything to keep out of Korea. I am beginning to think a guy could get killed over here. Ha! Ha!

I am enclosing an article that was in the "Stars & Stripes" (May 4) that you may be interested in reading. Recognize the outfit? That was the morning I got winged (April 23rd).

Am still at the Air Corp Hospital here in Nagoya. I eat like a pig. In fact I weigh 160 lbs. the most I have ever weighed.

Say 'Sul' how did your bowling do this season? Is Russ over here yet? I hope not. How's your family. All well I hope. Say is your Uncle still in Korea or is he in Japan. There is a fellow here in the hospital who knows who your uncle is. He is in the 7th reg 3rd div.

How's Ray Spear & Slim. Tell them to write. In fact tell anybody that wants to write to drop me a line. I'll answer. Especially women Ha! Ha!

Well will close for now. Want to get this into the 1:00 pick-up

'Cal'

Letter from Calvin to his Parents

May 9, 1951

Dear Folks,

Well I am still doing great here. I guess being in a hospital is doing me good. I weighed myself today and am up to 165 lbs. I guess it's the good food, plenty of sleep, (in bed at 9:30 up at 7:00) and very little exercise. I had my first dentist appointment yesterday and they filled my front teeth. Did a good job. Have another appointment tomorrow. By the time I get out of here I should have them all fixed.

Say do you know where Frank Careleo is in Korea. Could you call his house and find out what outfit he is in then send me the address. I've been wondering about it for quite some time and just never thought to ask about him when I was writting. Well there isn't much news here but I thought I would drop you all a line to let you know that I am doing great and will be out of here in no time (That's what I am afraid of Ha Ha!). Getting spoiled here I guess. Lots of Love to All

Cal

P.S. How's Foxy Grampa doing?

(This is Foxy Grandpa, the beloved cat that is referred to throughout this book.)

Letter from Ronald to Doris
9 May 51

Dear Aunt Doris,

Received your letter today and was really shocked to hear that "Cal" was wounded. I'm sure glad that it wasn't serious. I'll write to him tonight. Well, how are you all? Fine I hope. I am fine. The weather has been beautiful for the past few days and we expect to go swimming one day now. Oh, I must tell you. As of yet, the orders that will make me a Pfc. haven't come back from Nellis [Air Force Base] yet, they have been delayed, so I haven't been able to sew my stripes on. They expect the orders back any day now.

That fellow "Roland Ray" that you wrote me about is stationed at Nellis A.F. Base, not this base with me. I did go through basic with him and a lot of others from Springfield and Chicago. He is a swell kid. He pals around with a fellow named "Buddy" Arena, who enlisted with me in Westfield. You said that you have to move, well I sure hope that you can find a place because I understand that rents are pretty tough to find.

Well, I'll close now and go to chow before the "chow hands" start to gather at the door. Give my regards and love to Uncle Frank and Ann.

Love
Ronnie

("Air Force photograph: Scoring targets during the 1950 gunnery meet at Las Vegas Air Force Base." From Desert Lightning News, History of Nellis and Creech.)

Letters from Calvin to his Parents

May 14, 1951

Dear Mother & Dad,

Well they sewed me up today so I'll be just like new in know [no] time. At about 7:30 AM they gave me a shot of morfine [morphine]. That makes you sleepy and dopy. I guess it was 9:30 AM before they wheeled me up to the operating table. The 'Doc' stuck some kind of a needle into my throat. It makes you cough and puts a bitter taste in your mouth. I guess its so I wouldn't choke up or something, while they operated.

Ann can probably tell why they do that. Then the nurse gave me the needle in the right arm and I went out like a light. The next thing I knew I was resting comfortable on a bed back in the ward, a little dizzy but otherwise feeling great.

I received a letter from you Sat. (May 12th) Mom, and another one today. I also got one from Ann today. It was sure good to here [hear] from home again. The last time I got a letter was way back in March. Your last letter took only 6 days to get here at the hospital so I guess I should get mail more often now.

You were wondering what I got hit by. Well I think it was a bullet from a Chinese rifle or a Russian "burp" gun. There was so much lead flying I just couldn't tell. The slug just went in and out and that's all there was to it. It just felt like someone gave me a good sock in the shoulder. I think that Walter Donahue is OK. I was sorry to hear about Grandpa Clark. I hope that he is doing better by now. It makes it rough on a man his age. Glad to hear that Jimmie and Joan are getting married. They have been going around together for a long time. Hope you have a good time at the Conroy's Wedding.

Wish I could have been home to go to Ann's graduation. I kinda thought that she would get an award. She was always at the top of her class, even in school.

I see by your letter that you may have to move. I hope not. Don't let that guy downstairs sh___ on you. Well the lights are going out (9:30) so I will have to sign off for now.

Lots of Love
'Cal'

P.S. Tell Aunt Mable to go easy on the clam chowder. I sure want to thank 'Sully' for coming up to see you. A guy couldn't have a better friend than 'Sul'.

Am sending some pictures. A fellow in the ward with me took them. One was taken in Korea. The rest at the hospital here. He is not in my outfit.

(Written on the back of the photo by Calvin: "Taken on Hospital roof. Lousy picture. To much sun.")

("Taken on the roof of the hospital. The pants look kind of baggy don't they. They only have one size—to Big.")

("Taken on the roof of the hospital. Look one Hand")

(Taken in Korea:
"This was not the Mt.
I was on but it will
give you an idea of
the type of Terrain in
Korea. That smoke is
where a jelly bomb
just landed.")

("Taken from
hospital roof.
Those are
Japanese Kids
getting out of
school.")

May 25, 1951

Dear Mom & Dad,

Am writting from Camp Drake. From here I go to Sasebo and from there to my Co. in Korea. Have to go through here just like I did when I first left the states only this time I have two months to my credit in Korea. Leaving me four months at the most before I get rotated.

I think before to long they will come to some kind of settlement in Korea. It will take a week or better before I reach the Co. I was thinking maybe Russ Adams would be coming through here at the Camp soon. Maybe I'll see him.

While ridding here from Nagoya on the train, I met a fellow who used to work with me up to GE in Holyoke. His name is George Labonte. He is in the Navy and was on board some ship in Korea. He was on his way to the States and was hoping to be home soon. I was sure surprised to see him. Well there's not much news so I will close for now.

Lots of Love
To ALL
'Cal'

P.S. Best bet is to address your letters to the Co. now. I am in the best of shape and am none the worst for my experiences. Had a good rest in the hospital.

June 24, 1951

Dear Folks,

I'm writting from the western sector of South Korea some forty miles from the front. I am still with Co. K in the 57 recoilless rifle section. We expect to be here for quite a spell which doesn't hurt our feelings any. The time is really flying. It doesn't seem to me that I have been out of the hospital a month. In fact tomorrow will make 3 more in Korea with 3 to go. Everybody hopes it ends before then. The sooner the quicker!!

Was glad to here that you were moving even though it is a lot of work. Sounds like a good deal. Has many advantages over the old place which includes the neighbors downstairs. Of late the people downstairs we're never to [too] friendly compared to the ones we had when we first moved there. It should also be easier to keep clean.

Say, those strawberries sound good to me. Will be looking forward to some when I come home. Every time I mention something about you picking strawberries and making shortcakes and jam to the boys their eyes bug out and their mouths water. Incidentally so do mine!!!

I have received many letters since I have returned to the Co. It seemed good to hear from so many different people back home. Knowing that they were thinking of me makes a guy automatically feel better. Those were some writeups in the papers. They really poured it on. It was nice that Aunt Ruth can come up with some of the gang. Of course it would have to be at the same time as when you are moving. Maybe when I come home we can take a trip down there.

Am receiving mail very regular now. Just received a letter from you dated the 17th. Ann sure did good on those test. Say when is she going out with Frank Caroleo again. He writes to me and talks of her quite a lot. Am closing for now because the mail clerk is picking up the mail. But will write again soon now that we are in reserve.

Love Cal

P.S. There are some rumors of a cease fire over here soon. Sure hope so. Received a package from Grandma and Aunt Ellen. It was filled with cookies and Fruit Cocktail. A package came from you to the Co. while I was in the hospital. It had falling apart, so one of the boys that came with me from Cp. Devens ate it. Am still looking for the others.

Incidentally I am a Pfc. now since May 1 and may make Cpl. before I leave here.

Love Cal

[Pfc. is short for Private First Class and is the 3rd rank in the United States Army, ranking above Private Second Class and directly below a Specialist. Also note that when the editor asked Ann about Frank Caroleo, she replied, "Yes, I had a date with him. Very nice Italian guy. Didn't think he was interested in me. He was called to serve at Camp David. Then I met your dad (Norman) and we married and went to Alaska."]

June 30, 1951

Dear Mom & Dad,

Am still in the reserve area some ten miles below the 38th. We go swimming everyday. We have classes and inspections like back in basic also. Each Co. is having its day while we are here. Our day is July 4th. We will have ice cream, coke, cake, & etc. to eat & drink. There will also be competitive sports (softball, volleyball, horseshoes, & etc).

The weather has been ideal. Clear and hot, but cool at night. We hit the sack around ten except when there is a movie. Then we get to bed around 11:30.

I am getting quite a tan and am growing a cookie duster. It is quite the fad around here. *[A "cookie-duster" moustache is one that is thick and hangs over the upper lip. It looks as though it is capable of dusting off the cookie as you eat it.]*

Received the combat Inf. badge the other day. All those who have been in combat receive one. Have also been put in for the Purple Heart. I think it will help me out when rotation time rolls around (sometime in Sept.) It will make my hospital time count as time in Korea also.

You can never tell maybe we will be out of here before Sept. Heard this morning over the radio through a special news broadcast that General Ridgeway was going to meet with some Chinese General on the Danish ship the Jutlandia. That was the ship that I was on for a week before I went to Japan remember. By the time you receive this letter we will probably know how things are going to go one way or the other. Let's keep hoping and praying for a cease fire.

Not much more news. Thought I would try to drop a line to all the neighbors and friends who have written to me. Will write again soon

Love to all
Cal

P.S. Everything OK. Don't worry. Will be home before you know it.

(Green, Jonathon. Casell's Dictionary of Slang - 2nd Edition. Weidenfeld & Nicholson. 2005. Print)

July 31, 1951

Dear Folks,

Well here we are still in reserve much to our surprise. We've been here now since the 23rd of June. Except for a little moving around we have stayed in the same general area. While here we have been training and building bunkers (log covered foxholes) up in the hills. The cease-fire news doesn't change much from day to day. Don't know just what is going to happen. The Chinese are still building up along the front. But it is quite *[quiet]* all along the line.

Say have you received the money orders I sent home a couple of weeks ago? Let me know when you do. How's the moving coming along? Bet you'll be glad when it's done. How are things at the stand. Have there been any new additions to it?

Since we have been in reserve I have continued to put on a little weight. I have had a few pictures taken of myself and some of the boys in my squad. I am a gunner on the 57 mm recoilless rifle now. One fellow in the squad is an Indian from Utah, another is a Dutchman from Holland, and another is a South Korean named Chechun Soo. The squad leader is from California. Same UN outfit. I have been put in for Cpl. but have not got any word yet as to when I will make it. When you make a promotion over here you have to sign a statement to the effect that you will stay over here at least 30 days after you make your new rating. If I don't get it 30 days before I am due for rotation (Sept 25) I will refuse it. I think you will agree with me on this point. Although I am due for rotation the 25th of Sept. I do not expect to be rotated until my time, the first part of Oct. That's if conditions don't change over here. It could come sooner or later. There are only six of us who came into the Co. together who are due for rotation at that time (Sept 25). We will be the first ones on the U.S. list when it comes out (drafters) Maybe I'll be home for Thanksgiving or Christmas at the latest.

I saw the Jack Benny Show here about 3 weeks ago. *[July 7, 1951]* It was a pretty good show. He had Errol Flynn and actress Marjorie Reynolds with him. They put on a show for about an hour and a half.

We just learned tonight that our outfit along with the rest of the 3rd Bat. of the 32nd will receive the Presidential Unit citation for the battle on hill 902 on April 23rd. We get it Aug. 4th. Will close for now. Lots of Love to All

'Cal'

P.S. There is a shortage of envelopes here. They all get stuck down in this hot muggy weather. Send an envelope every time you write if you can. Put a piece of wax paper between the flap & the envelope.

P.S. (cont) Am enclosing a North Korean Bill. Thought you might like to see it. Tell Ann that I showed her picture to our 57 section leader and he has written her. His name is Robert Teague from Sidney, Ohio.

(A North Korean bill was enclosed in this letter, colored red with green.)

("Photo taken on July 7, 1951, Jack Benny and Errol Flynn entertaining the troupes in Korea." Chances are very good that this photo was taken of the same show Calvin is referring to in his previous letter home.)

(The above photograph and following article were published on January 29, 2018, at TheErrolFlynnBlog.com and written by Richard Iseri from Garden Grove California.)

INTERNET ARTICLES

trove.nla.gov...

Korean War Project
Salute Of Entertainers

Jack Benny and Company
(w/ 5th RCT, 24th Div.)

It was around the middle of July, 1951. The peace talks began earlier and there was peace in the Kumhwa valley.

Instead of combat, everyone was talking about rotating home. There was also a rumor about a USO troupe coming to this forward camp. During combat, we would see entertainers of two or three hitching rides to the rest areas, rain or snow, to give their little shows. I gave them a lot of credit for their courage. Bob Hope was also here for the troops but he was 50 miles behind us somewhere.

On this July day, the entertainers in trucks and jeeps, came driving into this little clearing. A makeshift stage was built for the occasion. To our surprise, It was none other than Jack Benny and with him, in the group was Errol Flynn and Marjorie Reynolds.

This is the first time I'd ever seen movie stars in the flesh. For this country boy, I was fascinated and they looked so human and of course, they were. On the stage, Jack did his comedy of jokes and Errol and Marjorie acted their series of mostly funny skits, a lot of laughs for all of us.

Everyone was standing around intermingling after the show. I was standing close to Jack. He somehow looked smaller than in the movies. I slowly sneaked up behind him and sure enough, I really was taller than he was!

Errol Flynn was walking by and I got this sudden impulse. I stuck out my hand and Mr. Flynn, can I shake your hand sir? He stopped, looked at me for a couple of seconds, smiled and said, My pleasure, lad, my pleasure. I think when he stopped and saw this oriental face, I can feel his uncertainty, but I think what won him over was this pure American slang coming from this face. He must have thought this guy has got to [be] a real Yankee.

(The above photograph and the one on page 118, along with the two following articles, were published on tralfaz.blogspot.com, on Sunday, January 12, 2014.)

ENTERTAINING IN THE KOREAN WAR ZONE

Bob Hope wasn't the only star who travelled around the world entertaining troops, though he's probably the first person you think of when the subject comes up. For example, Jack Benny toured during World War Two (including a stop in the oppressive summer heat in Iraq). He also made a jaunt to Korea during the conflict there.

To the right, [above] you see a picture dated June 26, 1951 of the Benny troupe. You should recognise at least one other face. In the far right of the photo is the formerly swashbuckling Errol Flynn, who died eight years later not too many blocks from where Jack's wife, Mary Livingstone, grew up in Vancouver's West End. To the far left is someone well-known to Benny fans—guitarist Frank Remley. Also in the photo are Benay Venuta, Marjorie Reynolds, tap dancer Dolores Gay, mentalist Harry Kahne and pianist June Bruner, who had been with Benny on a U.S.O. tour of the South Pacific during World War Two. The group returned home August 6th. He was cheery about the experience when he talked to the Associated Press' Hollywood reporter about the jaunt. The column appeared in newspapers on August 10, 1951.

JACK BENNY FINDS MORALE OF YANKS IN KOREA HIGH
By BOB THOMAS

Hollywood, Aug. 10 (AP)—"The morale of our men in Korea is terrific," reports Jack Benny, returned this week from entertaining troops in the front lines.

"They know what they're fighting for," added the fiddle-hacking comedian. "Naturally, they want peace. But they want the right kind of peace, and they're willing to continue fighting until they get it.

"The one thing that nearly every one of them asks is: 'Do the people back home know there's a war on?' I told them, 'You're darned right they do.'"

In his six weeks absence from Hollywood, Benny figures he traveled between 25,000 and 30,000 miles with his entertainment troupe. They played before troops and wounded veterans in Hawaii, Japan, Okinawa and throughout Korea. It was a thorough job. Virtually every possible audience of U. S. soldiers in the Orient was reached, with one exception. That was a group at Pusan who could not be reached because of bad landing conditions for aircraft.

"It was the toughest tour I ever made," said Benny, who made five world-wide journeys to entertain troops in World War II. "But also it was the most satisfying. I think we did the best job possible. Not only did we reach every audience we could, but we gave all the time possible to the other things that are important—posing for pictures with the GIs, signing autographs, talking and eating with the boys.

"The food was good wherever we went," said Benny. "But the living and traveling conditions were tougher than anywhere I had been, including North Africa. Much of the time I was living in a dirt-floor tent close to the front lines.

"We had to use every kind of transportation, from light aircraft to helicopter to jeep. The reason is because Korea is so mountainous. The boys have a gag over there that if Korea were flattened out, it would be as big as Texas."

Benny commented that his audiences were highly appreciative of the entertainment. They howled at any reference to Benny's alleged stinginess, such as: "That Tokyo is a fast town; I was there just a few days ago and 50 yen went just like that." As for his violin playing, "you'd think I was Heifetz."

Wherever he went, army bands would strike up "Love in Bloom." A navy base in Japan was filled with signs reading "Waukegan City Limits." As in the last war, there were occasional "Welcome Fred Allen" banners.

"There was only one audience from which we didn't get the laughs we usually got," he recalled. "They were a bunch of fellows who had to go out the next morning and take a hill which we could see from where we were. They were naturally uneasy, not because they were scared but because of the feeling that they might get hit with the peace possibly near."

Benny is urging other stars to enlist for entertainment in Korea. "It is the greatest audience in the world," he said.

"But it's a funny thing–they want good entertainment or none at all. They get fairly late movies and they like them if the pictures are good. If they're bad, the boys will walk out in the middle."

I asked Jack what gag got his biggest laugh.

"It was usually a local joke," he replied. "The best one was when I'd tell them I was going to retire and be a movie producer: "I can see it now–Jack Benny presents Bing Crosby and Bob Hope in 'The Road to Taegu'."

The United Press published a bit of a different take on the tour the following month. Jack admitted he was a little worn out by the whole experience. It wasn't like he was 39; he was 57 years old. But he didn't take it easy, either. He appeared in living rooms weekly for more than a dozen more years and performed benefit concerts and other charity events. He was beginning a movie comeback at the time of his death in 1974. But when the next war rolled around in Vietnam, Benny left the entertaining to others. One of them was Bob Hope. Ol' Ski Nose wasn't quite exhausted yet.

Letter from Calvin to his Parents

Aug. 21, 1951

Dear Mother & Dad,

Am receiving your letters regular. They only are taking from five to seven days to get here. Mine must be taking about two weeks to get to you.

We have moved from our old area since my last letter. We are near the line on "Division" reserved. In our last area we work in Coy reserve, But things are quite [quiet now] know on most of the line. Both sides are holding and building up with only a little partial [?] action. I guess I told you that if the ceasefire comes through we will be transferred to Japan.

Well I am in for Corporal and I signed last night. It will not effect my rotation. Incidentally they have a new rotation system of which you may have heard. It is a point system and covers all the Far East (Japan, Korea, etc) You get 4 points for each month you spend in Korea in a line outfit, 2 pts spent in a rear outfit per month and 1 pt. for each month you spend in Japan. Right now you are supposed to be rotated when you have 36 pts. But you can rotate anytime after you have 24 pts. At present I have 21 pts.

If you send packages send smaller ones but send them airmail. I know it is 'more expensive' but packages sent otherwise get here in terrible condition. That's if and when they reach here. I don't think I'll ever get all the packages you sent previously. The ones I did get were in rough shape and had been unwrapped. I know it is 'much more expensive' by airmail but the packages will get here exactly as you sent them and will get here as quick as your letters. Don't send candy because we get some here everyday in PX rations. Would rather have a couple of hometown newspapers or magazines (Readers Digest, Time, etc.) Cookies or hard candies keep good (Butterscotch) Particular cuss ain't I.

Say Ann's going pretty steady with Richie again, isn't she. *[Calvin is referring to Richard Doty; his photo is on page 122. His sister, Grace, wanted Ann to marry him, but when the editor asked Ann about it, she replied, "It wasn't meant to be."]*

If this ceasefire doesn't come through I believe that the fighting will not only continue here but will break out some other place to. The more places we have to send our troops without Russia having to use her troops the better she likes it. Hope this letter finds you all well. Lots of Love to All.

Cal

(Grace's brother, Richard Doty.)

Letter from Ronald to Doris and Franklin

"Pfc. Ronald W. Bein – A.F. 11204727"
[He must have received his stripes for "Pfc."]

23 Aug. 51

Dear Aunt Doris & Uncle Frank,

Well, at long last I am back to the old Air Force routine, and I hate it. My job in the control tower is being held by some other fellow and I am back on the ground crew. Also, my first day back, I was put on a detail by the sergeant that doesn't like me. I am going to see if I can get a transfer to some other base, or at least some other career field.

But putting that aside, I had a wonderful time while I was home. Right now I wish that I could have stayed there. It is rather hot here now and very dry. How is Ann? Fine I hope. Say hello to her for me. Well, I have lots of letters to write so I'll close for now.

Love to you all,
Ron [Bein]

Letters from Calvin to his Parents

Sept. 4, 1951
[Calvin becomes a Corporal.]

Dear Mom & Dad,

Received your letter dated Aug 25th. I am glad to here that they are going to have some sort of hockey in Springfield this season. Was sorry to here about Charlie Spaulding's mother and the Synch [?] girl. That automobile club sounds like fun.

Col. Charles M. Mount of which you speak used to be our Reg. Commander until about two months ago. He rotated. I don't know Sgt. Nelson but have heard of him. Incidently I am corporal now. It will not effect my rotation.

The weather here is about the same as it is back home. We are starting to have cool nights. Hope to get our field jackets and winter sleeping bags soon.

The days have been sunny and warm. Typical autumn weather. I hope I don't have to spend to many of the cold mons over here. The way rotation is going now I don't think I'll get rotated as soon as I thought. Although anything could happen over here. If the ceasefire came I might have got rotated sooner. You may read where they are rotating 30,000 a month over here. Sounds and reads good but it's a lot of "Bull _____." The most they are rotating is 7000. If it was 30,000 I would be on my way home now.

Say I see where my Giants aren't doing so bad. Would like to see them make it this year. Heard that Don Mueller of the of the Giants hit 4 home runs in two days.

["Mueller, who had been among the slumping hitters at the start of the year, hit very well in June and July. Of his 65 career home runs, five came in two consecutive games on September 1 and 2 against the Brooklyn Dodgers at the Polo Grounds, tying a record held by Adrian Anson, Ty Cobb, Tony Lazzeri, and Ralph Kiner." Society for American Baseball Research, Don Mueller, written by J. A. Petterchak. www.sabr.org.]

Just heard over the radio (one of the boys (8:55 AM here has a set) that Ridgeway called his ceasefire team back to Tokyo for a conference. I think you'll see the meetings start again and that the UN will give in some to the Chinese. If they don't the Chinese will just start another offensive and push us back over the 38th of which they are capable of doing after having all this time to build up. I don't think a certain Pres. or Secretary of State would like to see this war get any bigger but would rather see a halt to the fighting at least. It would be something for them to talk about at election time. All we can do is pray that everything turns out for the best. This is your 'Hoping to Rotate soon Son' closing for now and hoping that this letter finds you all in the best of health (lets not over work now) and spirits.

Love

Cal

P.S. Does Ann still think she'll go out West. Sounds like pretty good money. But is it worth it for such a short time. Would be good experience though.

Sept. 7, 1951

Dear Mom & Dad,

Received your letter postmarked the 31st last night. You know I completely forgot that it was your birthday mom [Aug. 29] but I do want to wish you a very happy birthday now even though it is a little late. I guess I have been thinking to much about rotation. I'll send you something when I get to Japan. Was glad to hear that you and Dad and Ann and Johnny went out and had a good time! We'll all have to hit those places when I get home. I am writting this letter by light from three bottles of bug repellent. We use rifle patches for wicks. Works pretty well. (Never use it for bugs.) (No bugs.)

We've seen a couple of Special Service shows recently and get a chance to see a movie once in a while. You'll also be glad to hear that I go to church services whenever it is possible. Which is more often than when I was home. Our Chaplin is from New Jersey and is very good. He is Protestant. I really must cut this letter short because it is getting late and we are getting up at 4:45. Not only that but I have pitched a tent with two Korean lads who are trying to sleep and keep reminding me to blow out the light and go to sleep-po. So will close for now

Lots of Love to all
Cal

Sept 26, 1951

Dear Mother & Dad,

Received your letters of Sept 12th and 16th. Also received the package you sent Sept 6th, 10 days ago. It was a swell package. It was enjoyed by all the other members of my squad also.

It seemed good to have some reading material. Am looking forward to the next package. I have just finished taking a shower and have received an issue of clean clothes. It sure makes a guy feel like a million dollars.

Action here has been quite [quiet] and I read in the Stars & Stripes where the Reds wanted to start the ceasefire talks again. It is hard to tell just what is going to happen next.

Rotation has started to pick up quite a lot. I think that I have a darn good chance of getting home before Christmas. Could be rotated some time the first part of Nov. I doubt if before.

There are quite a few fellows who came over with me that are staff sergeants now. You get ratings fast here. I would have been one (maybe) only my hospital time held me back. I don't care so much for the ratings anyway. I just want to rotate the hell out of here. Had six months over here yesterday. I figure I am over the hump and should be rotated sometime within the next two months. Hate like hell to spend the winter here.

Today I am celebrating my first year in the Army. Hope I am out a year from now.

Have noticed by your letters that you are putting quite a lot into the car. Hope it isn't costing you to much. Maybe I'll get a new one when I get out (Maybe!) I may send another money order home soon. This is your 'Hoping to Rotate Soon Son' closing for now. Lots of Love to All.

'Cal'

Oct 4, 1951

Dear Mom & Dad,

Received your letter of Sept 21st a few days ago. The fighting on our sector (east central) has been limited to patrols only at the present. Tomorrow (Oct 5th) we move off the line and go into reserve. We have been up here since Aug 9th. Our company commander said we should go into reserve for at least 40 days. I sure hope so because maybe I'll have a chance to rotate while I am in reserve.

I go on R&R (rest & recuperation) (Oct 5th) to Japan for five days not counting traveling time. At first they didn't want to let me go because I had had hospital time in Japan. It's a regimental [overly strict] policy not to let anyone with hospital time in Japan to go on R&R. But because I was there about 5 months ago they finally said I could go now. Boy I certainly bitched long enough. They were going to put my name at the end of the R&R list. I would have rotated before I would have got R&R.

Heard today that the N. Y. Giants had won the first playoff game against Brooklyn. Hope they win the pennant.

Not much more news. Will write again from Japan.

Lots of Love To all
'Cal'

Oct 14, 1951

Dear Mom & Dad,

Well I finally got some pictures taken of myself. Wiskers [whiskers] and all. They were taken the last time we were on the line. The Chinese in one of the pictures was about thirty-five years old. He just walk [walked] into our lines and gave up. He said that most of his outfit had been killed. I guess he had had enough.

In one of the pictures I am sitting with a fellow who was in my company back at Devens. He is Jack Fazzino from N.Y. City. He is now a platoon sgt. in the company. We call him 'Fuzzi.' The two bigger pictures I had taken in a studio in Yokohama, Japan while I was on R&R. As you can see I got rid of the wiskers.

While I was on R&R I bought a couple of items which I thought you might be able to use and would also look good in the house. You probably won't get them for a period of three to six weeks. I also sent Sully & Carol something for their first wedding anniversary. I see Sully isn't wasting much time.

Say the Giants really made a great finish. That was some home run by Bobby Thompson. I guess they just ran out of steam during the World Series. To Bad.

Say Dad that's a darn good picture of the Water Wheel. When did you have Post Cards made of it? Hey Dad, you had a birthday back a few days ago didn't you? Bet you thought I'd forgot. Happy Birthday!! Say how old did you say you were. Over fifty wasn't it.

I am looking forward to rotation soon. I can't say just how soon. But I hope I am home for Christmas. We'll keep our hope up and keep praying anyway.

Well I think I'll turn in and get a little shut-eye

Love to all
Cal

P.S. Our outfit is in Reserve now. In the same area that we were in back in July.

(ABOVE: J. Calvin Coolidge with his "cookie duster" mustache sitting in a trench alongside Jack Fazzino. BELOW: Photo of the water wheel mentioned in letter, purchased by Franklin in the fall of 1950 from George Gale.)

THE SPRINGFIELD UNION, SPRINGFIELD, MASS., FRIDAY

HAND-HEWN WATER WHEEL—West Springfield Oct. 11—Formerly on the George Gale farm in Petersham, the wheel shown in the background of the above picture, was purchased by "Doc" Coolidge of the Valley Farms fruit stand here two years ago. The hand-hewn, wooden wheel was carefully taken apart and carted to its present site, where it has been reassembled next to a barn in a picturesque atmosphere.

The wheel formerly pumped water 1300 feet with a rise of 100 feet on a brook on the Gale farm. It was replaced with an electric pump. It is eight feet in diameter, has 35 buckets, and turns with only a small trickle of water. Even the original water spout was bought by Coolidge and reassembled.

In addition to the old water wheel, a wellsweep was found in the Petersham district, now the site of Quabbin Reservoir, which has been rebuilt in front of the water wheel. On the Page farm in New Salem, an old split rail fence was found, and part of it was obtained by Coolidge to go with the rest of his antiques.

(ABOVE: A newspaper article that Calvin's parents mailed to him in one of their letters. The article is dated October 13, 1950, and was published in The Springfield Union paper. For your convenience, the article is typed below.)

HAND-HEWN WATER WHEEL—West Springfield, Oct. 11—Formerly on the George Gale farm in Petersham, the wheel shown in the background of the above picture, was purchased by "Doc" Coolidge of the Valley Farms fruit stand here two years ago. The hand-hewn, wooden wheel was carefully taken apart and carted to its present site, where it has been reassembled next to a barn in a picturesque atmosphere.

The wheel formerly pumped water 1300 feet with a rise of 100 feet on a brook on the Gale farm. It was replaced with an electric pump. It is eight feet in diameter, has 35 buckets, and turns with only a small trickle of water. Even the original water spout was bought by Coolidge and reassembled.

In addition to the old water wheel, a wellsweep was found in the Petersham district, now the site of Quabbin Reservoir, which has been rebuilt in front of the water wheel. On the Page farm in New Salem, an old split rail fence was found, and part of it was obtained by Coolidge to go with the rest of his antiques.

Oct 27, 1951

Dear Mom & Dad

Have received your last two letters dated the 11th & 15th of Oct. Was glad to hear that everybody was O.K.

I don't know where Frank Caroleo got the idea that I was going to Japan on my way home. But I am not. Not yet anyway. But I expect to be on my way soon. The way I see it I could rotate anytime within the next 8 weeks.

I told him that I was going on R&R to Japan. That stands for Rest and Recuperation. You get 5 or six days there to do as you please. More or less just a 5 day pass. What do you think of the pictures I sent? Glad to hear that Ann is taking guitar lessons. I must close this letter for now because the mailman is taking the mail and I want this letter to get on its way so as to explain the situation to you. Will right [write] a longer letter soon.

Love to all
Cal

Oct 28, 1951

Dear Mom & Dad,

Received your letter postmarked Oct 18th this morning. Don't blame Frank for misinterpreting the letter that I wrote him because in the letter I said I was going on R&R to Japan and then a little latter [later] in the letter I told him to save some beer for me when I get home. I am glad it has all been straightened out now however. If he calls at the house again you can tell him to leave the beer <u>on the ice</u> because I will be home soon, I hope.

They rotated nine men from the Company this week and I think that will put me somewhere around twenty on the rotation list.

I was sorry to hear about Mrs. Bradley. She must have suffered a lot. Tell 'Sully' to write when he gets a chance. I have written him two letters and haven't heard from him yet.

I got back from R&R just a couple of days after the typhoon "Ruth" hit Japan. I was kinda hoping it would hit while I was there because all planes were grounded and I would have had three more days in Japan. Japan seems like <u>heaven</u> compared to this place. I can't imagine what the 'States' and home will seem like. I now [know] it will seem darn good. That's for sure!! That's for dang sure!!!

Was glad to hear that Grandpa Clark was feeling good.

That last package you sent was great. Tell Ann that she's a good 'cooker.' The boys, along with myself enjoyed the package very much. I got it just before I went on R&R. Will close for now.

Lots of Love to All
'Cal'

Nov 9, 1951

Dear Mom & Dad,

Received your letter dated Oct 25th and Oct 30th. Glad you liked the pictures. I thought you'd get a good laugh out of my "cookie duster."

Glad to hear that you both are going to take a vacation. What are you planning on doing? It is good that you are saving some money. It always comes in handy. I am sending another $100.00 money order with this letter. Let me know when you receive it.

We have received our winter clothing [note date, Nov 9]. I think, for the present anyway, that they have given us to much clothes.

The weather here has been rather cold. The ground is frozen in the morning but thaws out during the day. We had about 2 inches of snow the other night but it all melted during the day.

Rotation has picked up a lot recently. I am about no. 15 on the companies [company's] rotation list. But I don't think I'll rotate much before a month or six weeks. Although you never can tell.

I am squad leader now in the first squad of 57s. I have charge of the squad (about six men) and do not have to carry or fire the weapon anymore. The job calls for staff-sgt. but I would have to sign for 30 more days and I am to close to rotation to take a chance on signing.

The 57 recoilless rifle is not a bazooka. The principle of both is the same. But mechanicly they are very different. The effective range with the bazooka is 300 yds. while with the 57 it is 1200 yds. We do fire at a greater distance than this however.

There's not much more news. Will write again soon.

Lots of Love to All
'Cal'

Nov 23, 1951

Dear Mom & Dad,

Received your letters dated Nov 3rd & 6th. Was glad to hear that you liked the gifts I sent from Japan.

Chaplin Frost is the chaplin [chaplain] in our outfit (3rd Bat.) I go to his services whenever I get a chance. He is a good speaker. I doubt if I was in that picture though.

Yesterday we celebrated Thanksgiving with a turkey dinner. The menu was as follows.

Turkey	Pie	Corn
Salad	Cake	Mixed Nuts
Shrimp Cocktail	Potatoes	Hard Candy
Squash	Bread	Apple & Orange
Cranberry Sauce	Olives	

Last night we had about four inches of snow. The ground isn't frozen though and as soon as the sun came out it started to melt. As far as winter clothes are concerned we have got plenty. In fact I think we've got to much. Here is a list of our winter clothes.

Woolen Underwear	Woolen sweater
" " OD Shirt	Field Jacket
" " Pants	Pile " & Cap.

Field Pants (over OD Pants)
Parka (3/4 coat with a wool lines and a fur hood)
Gloves (Woolen inserts & leather shells)

We also have a winter sleeping bag. They are made of feathers and keep you very warm.

About ten days ago I saw the Danny Kaye Show with Monica Lewis. It was a darn good show. There was also a girl with the show who played the accordion and sang. She was with the Jack Benny show last summer. One of the songs she sang which I liked best was "Because of You." *[The editor believes the cast consisted of: Danny Kaye, Monica Lewis, June Bruner, who I believe played the accordion, and Sam Praeger. They were photographed in Los Angeles on November 21st getting off of a plane together.]*

I am still hoping to rotate by "Christmas" and am hoping the cease-fire comes through. Will close for now.

Lots of Love to All, 'Cal'

(This photograph and following write up is from the Facebook page, "Monica Lewis Tribute.")

THANKSGIVING, KOREA, NOVEMBER 1951: Recalled Monica of this very special celebration of the holiday: "Before departing South Korea at the end of my nearly month-long troop-entertainment tour of the frontlines with my friend and fellow performer Danny Kaye, I helped prepare, serve and celebrate a Thanksgiving feast with the 14th Infantry Regiment -- also known as the Lightning Lynx -- which adopted me into its ranks. As I left the regiment's command post for the last time, I cried as I read the carefully handmade sign over the entrance: 'The Home of Lightning Lynx and Monica Lewis.' I have never forgotten these soldiers, their sacrifices or their wonderful, courageous spirit. Let us give thanks to all our brave men and women in uniform -- and their families -- throughout U.S. history who have secured the foundation upon which we have built our dreams. #HappyThanksgiving! Love always, Monica"

("Monica Lewis sings for the troops during her November 1951 tour of the KoreanWar frontlines with fellow performer DannyKaye." Posted on the Monica Lewis Tribute Twitter page.)

(Monica Lewis and Danny Kaye 1951 tour for the Korean troops.)

("CPL Mervyn Lew, photographer. Comedian Danny Kaye Entertains Troops of the 5th RCT, 24th U.S. Infantry Division, during Show Held Near Kumsong, Korea, November 6, 1951. Photograph. Music Division, Library of Congress.")

Letters from Calvin to his Parents

Nov 28, 1951

Dear Mom & Dad,

Things here are about the same. It's been cold here for quite a few days. We had about four inches of snow a couple of days after Thanksgiving Day.

It is quite [quiet] on most of the front. I hope the new agreement on where the cease-fire line should be while they work on the other armistice points will keep it quite [quiet]. But you can never tell what these Chinese will do or just what they are up to.

I am no. nine on the Co. rotation list and hope to be on my way home by the first of the year.

I received your fruit cake yesterday. It was swell. Did you all have a good Thanksgiving? I could just picture all the good things you had to eat. We didn't do to bad here but there's nothing like good old home cooking.

Tell Ann to keep up on those guitar lessons. I am anxious to hear her play. Can she play 'Steel Guitar Rag'? [Written by Bob Wills.]

I still haven't heard from Sully. But mail has been getting here rather slow lately so that may be it. With this bad weather the planes are grounded and makes the mail late.

Will write again soon. Before you know it I'll be rotating and will be on my way home. Yippee!!

Love "Cal"

Dec 7, 1951

Dear Mom & Dad,

Have received your letters postmarked November 20 & 25. In this letter I am sending you another Money Order for you to put into the bank for me. Let me know when you receive it. Say how much money do I have in the bank now anyway?

They have given us Christmas cards (about 10) to send home to our folks & friends. You will receive your card along with this letter I imagine because I am mailing them together. Am sending one to Mr. Wallace and his family. *[Wallace was the Coolidge family's Minister at the Baptist Church in West Springfield. He baptized Calvin and Ann by emersion.]*

I have written Sully & Carol but haven't heard from them yet. Will write to them again today. I am sending them a card also. Also sending one to Ann. Haven't received the package yet that you spoke of sending in your Nov 25 letter. But ought to get it soon. I imagine the mails are jammed.

The weather here hasn't been to cold. At the present time however it is snowing very hard. I never minded cold weather much anyway. Some of the G.I.'s over here mind the cold though.

Not much to write about. Everybodies still hoping for the cease-fire. Things are quite [quiet] along most of the front. Sure hope it comes soon. Will close for now. Merry Christmas & a Happy New Year.

Lots of Love to All
'Cal'

Dec. 15, 1951

Dear Mom & Dad,

Received your letter dated the 2nd & 6th of Dec. Was glad to hear that you have sent a package. They are always welcomed over here.

I was glad Dad got my license renewed. Was surprised though that it cost more. Prices must be really climbing back home especially taxes. You know the saying "You can't take it with you." Well the way taxes are climbing I don't think anyone can afford to go.

Things over here haven't changed much since the cease-fire talks started up again back in Oct. Our company commander (better known as the 'CO' or 'Old man!') told us last night that Higher Headquarters (Army) thinks that this time they will sign the cease-fire. I believe that when and if the cease-fire is signed it will come all of a sudden. Because right now the Chinese are causing a stalemate and will until the last minute to try and get all they can from of us.

We relieved the Second Division on 'Heartbreak Ridge' last Oct 20th and we are now in reserve. Came down the 10th of Dec. We were the only Battalion in the 7th Division that spent 50 straight days on the line without any reserve. We expect to be down on reserve now for quite a spell.

I got some more Christmas cards and will send some out as soon as I can. Don't think they will arrive in time for Christmas but they ought to get there for New Years. The thought is there anyway.

There isn't much news. Before closing I want to wish you all a Very Happy New Year.

Love to All
Cal

P.S. I hope to be leaving soon.

(Nothing was written on the back of this photo, but Calvin appears to be standing in the back, fourth from the left.)

THIRTY SECOND INFANTRY REGIMENT
APO 7

Dec. 20, 1951

Dear Mom & Dad,

Received your letter dated the 10th of Dec.

I got a Christmas Card from Russell Adams yesterday and he said that he was in Korea and had been here since the 5th of Dec. He is in the 180th Inf. Regt. I think it is part of the 40th Div. that has been stationed in Japan for some time and is now coming to Korea possibly to relieve some Divs. over here. There are rumors, and they are strictly rumors, that the 7th Div. may get relieved. For the 7th Div. has had more line time than any other Div. in Korea.

Our company is still in reserve. We are guarding a radar installation that directs all bombing missions in Korea. All the way to the Manchurian border. Just across the river here they are building an air strip that when it is finished will be the biggest air strip in Korea. It will be used for bombers (B-29's or jets).

Got a card from Dewen Chambelin the other day. It was a wallet type card and had $2 in Stateside money in it. That was very thoughtful of her I thought since I hadn't written her.

I am enclosing some pictures that I thought you might be interested in seeing. I don't like the picture of me (one with rabbit ears). There are two of the 57. As you can see in one of them it had just snowed. When the 57 is set up like this it can hit any target within 2000 yds. with pin point accuracy. Incidentally it is pointed directly at Joe 'Chink.' We were firing mostly from 1100 to 1600 yds. The other picture is one taken of our First Sgt. and a fellow who came over here with me from Deven. His name is 'Art' Costello. He is from New Jersey. I will probably rotate with him. The one on the right is 'Art.'

We are going to have a Co. Christmas party here on the night before Christmas. Don't know just what we'll do. I guess we'll sing Christmas Carols. Eats and drinks will be furnished by the Battalion (bless their hearts). I know will all be thinking of home and wishing we were there. That's for sure!! That's for Dang sure!!!

Oh well maybe I'll be rotating soon and we can all have a Christmas & New Years party rolled up in one. What a party. The weather here has been warm for this time of year. Will close for now.

Lots of love to all
'Cal'

December 25, 1951
Yangju, Korea
8:00 PM

[Yangju is a city in South Korea not far from Seoul, south of Dongducheon and north of Uijeongbu.]

Dear Mom & Dad,

Well Christmas is just about over here. But it's just starting back home. Had a swell dinner. The menu was the same as Thanksgiving Day. Haven't received any packages yet but expect to soon.

It started to snow about 10:00 AM today and is still snowing. Have about 6–8 in. now.

There's a fellow in the 57's who is from Hawaii and plays the guitar. So Christmas Eve he played and some of us gathered around and sang Carols. Sure made us homesick. Also sang some popular songs. The sgts. got their wiskey [whiskey] rations so the party never got cold. The rest of us got five cans of beer a piece.

Well to-day I have nine months in Korea. I hope the hell I am rotated before my tenth month is up. I've been saying that now for four months. To-morrow I'll have 15 months in the Army. Still don't know whether I've got to spend 21 or 24 mons. in this mans Army. Maybe you've got some information on this subject. If so pass it on.

Well by the time you get this letter Christmas & New Years will be over but I hope you all get what you've asked for and that your stocking's are overflowing.

Not much news thing's are about the same. Still hoping for a cease-fire. Will close for now

Lots of Love To All
Cal

P.S. Are you all having a getogether around Christmas or New Years?

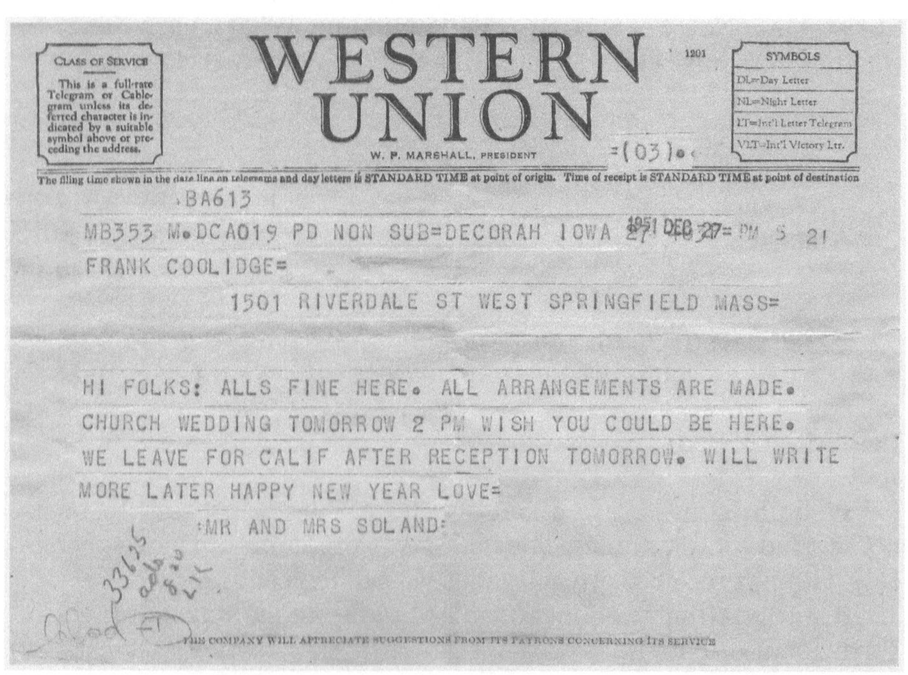

WESTERN UNION

W. P. MARSHALL, PRESIDENT

CLASS OF SERVICE
This is a full-rate Telegram or Cablegram unless its deferred character is indicated by a suitable symbol above or preceding the address.

SYMBOLS
DL=Day Letter
NL=Night Letter
LT=Int'l Letter Telegram
VLT=Int'l Victory Ltr.

1201

=(03)

The filing time shown in the date line on telegrams and day letters is STANDARD TIME at point of origin. Time of receipt is STANDARD TIME at point of destination

BA613

MB353 M.DCA019 PD NON SUB=DECORAH IOWA 27 1951 DEC 27 PM 5 21

FRANK COOLIDGE=

1501 RIVERDALE ST WEST SPRINGFIELD MASS=

HI FOLKS: ALLS FINE HERE. ALL ARRANGEMENTS ARE MADE. CHURCH WEDDING TOMORROW 2 PM WISH YOU COULD BE HERE. WE LEAVE FOR CALIF AFTER RECEPTION TOMORROW. WILL WRITE MORE LATER HAPPY NEW YEAR LOVE=

MR AND MRS SOLAND=

THE COMPANY WILL APPRECIATE SUGGESTIONS FROM ITS PATRONS CONCERNING ITS SERVICE

WESTERN UNION
TELEGRAM SENT 12/27/51

BA613
MB353 M.DCA019 PD NON SUB=DECORAH IOWA 27
FRANK COOLIDGE=
1501 RIVERDALE ST WEST SPRINGFIELD MASS=

HI FOLKS: ALLS FINE HERE. ALL ARRANGEMENTS ARE MADE. CHURCH WEDDING TOMORROW 2 PM WISH YOU COULD BE HERE. WE LEAVE FOR CALIF AFTER RECEPTION TOMORROW. WILL WRITE MORE LATER HAPPY NEW YEAR LOVE=

MR AND MRS SOLAND

(This photo was taken on December 24, 1941, four days before Ann and Norman were married. Ann had just met the family. Back row: Norman, and his brothers Eugene and Robert. Front row: Robert's wife June, Ann, Norman's father Embret who is holding Julie, Norman's mother Louise holding Joan, James, and Ernest's wife Julia.)

[Norman later looked back on the telephone conversation when he asked Ann's parents permission to marry her, in a letter dated October 10, 1959. He wrote to Doris, Frank & Cal, *"Was telling Ann how glad I was we didn't wast [waste] any more time than we did when we got married. Got to thinking of that nite we called you for permission—Golly it must have been rough. Hope I can be as understanding as you both were that nite, & still are. I'm becoming aware of how much grief young ones can cause older people with no concern or feeling. As I am sure our phone call did that night for you two. Guess you both would have stomped your feet & said no—We would have still gotten married & had our five children—But that night—your not knowing—Sure got to look up to you—& no fooling there."*]

SOLAND AND COOLIDGE

[Actual newspaper article on page 159.]

Sgt. and Mrs. Norman Soland are pictured above following their wedding Friday afternoon. Dec. 28, at the Washington Prairie Lutheran church. The 2 o'clock ceremony was performed by Rev. O. E. Engebretson.

The bride is the former Ann Coolidge, daughter of Mr. and Mrs. Franklin P. Coolidge, of West Springfield, Mass., and Sgt. Norman Soland is the son of Mr. and Mrs. Embret Soland of Decorah.

Rev. O. E. Engebretson officiating with the double ring ceremony. Mrs. O. E. Engebretson played the wedding marches and accompanied Miss Marilyn Sersland, who was soloist.

The bride wore a white brocaded satin gown styled with sweetheart neckline and court train. Her fingertip veil was held by a tiara of orange blossoms, and she carried a bouquet of yellow roses with mixed pompons.

Mrs. Ernest Soland, attending her as matron of honor, wore a blue satin gown and carried a bouquet of pink roses and pompons. The bridegroom was attended by his brother, Ernest Soland, and ushers were Eugene Soland and Roy Nesheim.

After the ceremony 60 guests were received at the Green Parrot.

Mrs. Soland is a 1951 graduate of the New England Baptist Hospital, Boston. Mr. Soland has been serving in the United States Air Force for the past year. He spent last year as an instructor at Chanute Field, Ill., and has since been transferred to Alaka [Alaska] where his wife will join him.

(Sgt. and Mrs. Norman Soland, married December 28, 1951, at Washington Prairie Lutheran Church in Decorah, Iowa.)

(Norman's great-grandfather donated the land for the Washington Prairie Lutheran Church, and the parsonage was dedicated on December 17, 1873. The Soland family farm is located adjacent to the church and is operated by Mark Soland, Norman's brother Ernest's son. The Washington Prairie Lutheran Church website states, "In 1949, the Washington Prairie Congregation was voted one of the twelve great churches in America according to a poll conducted by Christian Century of 100,000 pastors.")

(Norman Jerome Soland in his Air Force uniform.)

(Following WWII, the Soviet Union blocked routes into West Berlin that were used to transport desperately needed supplies that the Germans needed to survive. So, the United States and other Western allies organized an airlift of goods that were delivered into the center of the city of Berlin. Norman Soland flew that airlift as "Crew Chief Engineer." When I asked Norman, my father, what he actually did, he replied, "I made sure that the plane flew." He explained that they were landing an airplane in the center of town one every minute, and the landing gear, or wheels of the plane, would just miss hitting the tops of the buildings as they were retracted.)

(A postcard of Chanute Air Force base where Norman spent a year as an instructor prior to meeting Ann. Chanute is located in Champaign County, Illinois, about 130 miles south of Chicago.)

(Ann Soland, Norman's 92 year-old grandmother Gunhilda E. Arness [maiden name, Ramsey], and Norman Soland. Photo taken on Gunhilda's couch in her home in the town of Decorah, Iowa.)

[*Ann and Norman were married in Decorah, Iowa, on December 28, 1951. Their reception was held at The Green Parrot Restaurant, then they drove to Norman's brother Bob's house in Jesup, Iowa, where they spent their wedding night. The following day they headed for Camp Stoneman in California where they would wait for three weeks for Norman's orders overseas. Ann and Norman had heard that Calvin would soon to be on his way home, and hoped to see him at Camp Stoneman, but Calvin came through after they had left. Norman received his orders for Alaska and traveled there by boat. Ann could not go with him because they had no place to live. She stayed in Seattle for seven weeks with Norman's Aunt, Emilia Guttebo, while Norman found a place for them to live in Fairbanks, Alaska.*]

(The new couple held their reception in a private dining room at The Green Parrot on State Road. The owners, Les and Ruth Branhagen, were friends of the Solands. Their farm was down the road from the Red Oak school, not far from the Soland family farm. The original owner, Bertha Nesheim, claimed that it was the "finest eating place in this territory.")

(Vintage postcard of The Green Parrot Restaurant in Decorah, Iowa.)

(Ann and Norman preparing to leave for California the morning of December 29, 1951. The photo was taken in front of June and Bob Soland's house in Jesup, Iowa. Bob was Norman's brother.)

1952

(Ann "Coolidge" Soland stands in front of the Shell Motel where Norman and Ann stayed while at Camp Stoneman, Pittsburg, California. They were waiting for Norm's orders to go "overseas," which ended up being Alaska. The "X" marks the room in which they slept.)

(Norman Soland in his Air Force uniform at Camp Stoneman. He must not have wanted his picture taken; he's sticking out his tongue.)

(Western Union telegram dated January 7, 1952)

WESTERN UNION
[Telegram sent January 7, 1952 at 1:46 pm.]

BA820 OB463
O.CSA226 NLPD=CAMP STONEMAN CALIF 7=
MR FRANK COOLIDGE=
1501 RIVERDALE ST SPRINGFIELD MASS=

DEAR FOLKS. ALLS FINE. WRITE CAL. THAT WE ARE HERE. FOR HIM TO WIRE US. IF HE SHOULD COME SOON. WILL BE AT THIS ADDRESS POSSIBLY TWO WEEKS, GUEST HOUSE CAMP STONEMAN CALIF, MISS YOU ALL MUCH DO TAKE GOOD CARE OF ANN FOR ME, LOVE=

NORM AND ANN=..

Letters from Calvin to his Parents

Jan 10, 1951 [Calvin meant 1952.
Envelope is postmarked "1952."]
Inchon, Korea
9:15 P.M.

Dear Folks,

Just dropping you a few lines to let you know that I am on my way home. Yes believe it or not I am finally rotating.

All of us that came into the Company together are also rotating together. I still can hardly believe it. Left the company the morning of the eighth and expect to leave this port (Inchon) by boat for Sasebo in Japan in the next couple of days. Don't look for me though much before the 10th of Feb. I imagine it will take about 30 days to get home. Will write again soon. Just thought I'd let you know I was on the way.

Love
Cal

19 / Jan / 52
Sasebo, Japan

Dear Mom & Dad,

Just a couple of lines to let you know that we are leaving tomorrow for the States. It will take about two weeks going across the ocean. So I should be home in about three weeks. We will either dock in Seattle or San Francisco and from there by train to the camp nearest your home. So I will have to go to Ft. Devens before coming home. And then I will have a 30 day furlough. Will close for now.

Love
'Cal'

PS. See you all in three weeks

Thursday, January 31, 1952
West Springfield News
VOL. XXV, No. 6

Cpl. Coolidge
Home From Korea

WITH THE 7th INFANTRY DIV. IN KOREA– John C. Coolidge, son of Mr. and Mrs. Franklin P. Coolidge, 1501 Riverdale St., West Springfield, Mass., is returning home under the Army's rotation policy after serving with the 7th Division on the Korean fighting front.

During recent action the division has been attacking Communist positions in the snow-covered mountains north of the 38th Parallel. The 7th has been playing a major role in the Korean war since landing at Inchon in September, 1950.

Coolidge, who served as a 57-mm recoilless rifle squad leader with the 32nd Inf. Regt., entered the Army Sept. 26, 1950. He wears the Korean Service Ribbon with two campaign stars, the Presidential Unit Citation Emblem and the Combat Infantryman Badge.

WEST SPRINGFIELD

VOL. XXV, NO. 6 — WEST SPRINGFIELD (MASS.) THURSDAY, JANUARY 31, 1952

Cpl. Coolidge Home From Korea

WITH THE 7TH INFANTRY DIV. IN KOREA—Cpl. John C. Coolidge, son of Mr. and Mrs. Franklin P. Coolidge, 1501 Riverdale St., West Springfield, Mass., is returning home under the Army's rotation policy after serving with the 7th Division on the Korean fighting front.

During recent action the division has been attacking Communist positions in the snow-covered mountains north of the 38th Parallel. The 7th has been playing a major role in the Korean war since landing at Inchon in September, 1950.

Coolidge, who served as a 57-mm recoilless rifle squad leader with the 32nd Inf. Regt, entered the Army Sept. 26, 1950. He wears the Korean Service Ribbon with two campaign stars, the Presidential Unit Citation Emblem and the Combat Infantryman Badge.

PTA Council's Founder Day

The West Springfield-Agawam PTA Council will hold its annual Founders' Day observance next Wednesday evening at John Ashley school with a program scheduled to open at 7:45. All units of the two towns will participate, and any other interested residents are also cordially invited to attend.

Guest speaker for the evening is to be Officer Rudy Zbonchak, of the West Springfield Police Department. Officer Zbonchak

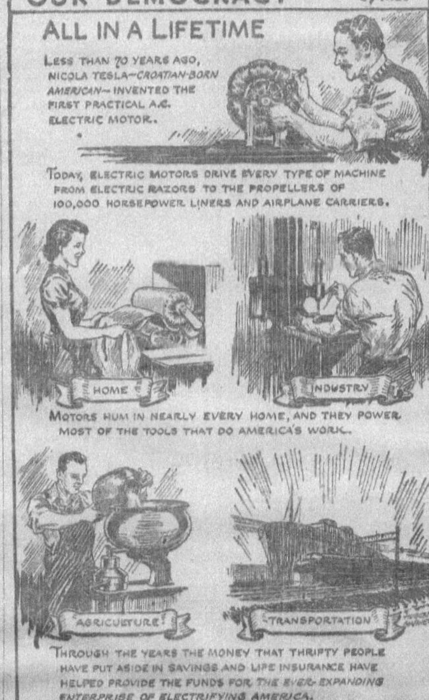

Township Re[...] In

Fellow townsmen wh
present at the John As
dedication the other n
share the spirit of th
just the same. It was
experience that belon
whole community.

The John Ashley cer
the first of three—and
— of the same whic
ahead for West Spring
spiring fruition of yea
and planning by many
bring our education
to date.

**Why inspiring? B
represents that en
outlook whereby on
tion seeks to make
community for the g
to come, and becau
a milestone in the h
West Springfield,
that mid-century w
community became
over its school situ
aroused that it spen
of its substance to
build.**

Supt. Stanley Wrigh
John Ashley dedicatio
priate perspective by h
recognition of the man
zens whose efforts br
the school building p
one educator, no one
ing, no single group
ble for the new Jo
school.

It was a dream of

Citizen Says [...] Brings

To the Editor:

(January 31, 1952, "Cpl. Coolidge Home From Korea")

Letter from Ann to her Parents

Mrs. N. J. Soland
c/o Mrs. Emilia Guttebo
12231 Roseburg South
Seattle 88, Wash.

[postmarked Feb. 13, 1952]
February 13th Wednesday [1952]
Norm's address (same name & serial no.
10th Air Reserve Sgdn. D=Felt.
APO 713 c/o Postmaster
Seattle, Wash.

Dear Folks,

Just a line to let you know we are all fine here in Seattle, except I have a slight cold right now.

Didn't mean to break down on the phone, but it seemed so good to hear Cal's voice again.

Norm left yesterday for Fairbanks–got a wire about 9 AM. Said he will call me on Thurs., Feb. 14.

I got 4 letters too and long ones. He is very lonesome too and wants me to come up just as soon as he can find us a place. He had not received any mail at all. Said that the Government will ensure me a "Parka" and boots, like Dale had. It must be pretty cold up there – about 60 below zero. Right in the Arctic Circle. He will be stationed at Ladd Field. He will be flying emergency—picking up expectant mothers, lost persons etc. It doesn't sound very good, but said it would only be for a while. Said he will also have homework to do.

I wrote to the Nurses Assoc. in Alaska, and also to Miss Pekrul. *[She was the administrator of N.E. Baptist Hospital.]* If I have a position I can just step into, I may be able to get up there sooner.

Our wedding picture was in the Decorah paper. Sent it to Norm. Norm's mother will probably send you one.

Hope everything is all well at home. I bet Carol is going ice skating. I haven't been at all this year. How's Foxy Grandpa? How did you like the carriage deal, Cal? Some smart cat! Will call you if anything turns up.

Love,
Ann ["Coolidge" Soland]

[Ann got a job working as a nurse in a gynecology clinic in Fairbanks, Alaska, where pregnant women came to be examined by their doctor.]

MR. AND MRS. NORMAN J. SOLAND
Whose recent marriage in Decorah, Ia., is announced. The bride was formerly Miss Ann Coolidge of West Springfield.

Ann Coolidge Wed To Norman Soland

Ceremony Performed in Decorah, Ia.

Mr. and Mrs. Franklin P. Coolidge of West Springfield, announce the recent marriage of their daughter, Ann, to Sgt. Norman J. Soland, son of Mr. and Mrs. Embert Soland of Decorah, Ia. The marriage took place in the Washington Prairie Lutheran Church, Decorah, Rev. O. E. Engebretson officiating with the double ring ceremony. Mrs. O. E. Engebretson played the wedding marches and accompanied Miss Marilyn Sersland, who was soloist.

The bride wore a white brocaded satin gown styled with sweetheart neckline and court train. Her fingertip veil was held by a tiara of orange blossoms, and she carried a bouquet of yellow roses with mixed pompons.

Mrs. Ernest Soland, attending her as matron of honor, wore a blue satin gown and carried a bouquet of pink roses and pompons. The bridegroom was attended by his brother, Ernest Soland, and ushers were Eugene Soland and Roy Nesheim.

After the ceremony 60 guests were received at the Green Parrot.

Mrs. Soland is a 1951 graduate of the New England Baptist Hospital, Boston. Mr. Soland has been serving in the United States Air Force for the past year. He spent last year as an instructor at Chanute Field, Ill., and has since been transferred to Alaka where his wife will join him.

Newspaper Article
Feb. 21, 1952

NORTH NEW SALEM

Cpl. Calvin Coolidge, son of Mr. and Mrs. Franklin Coolidge of West Springfield, who has recently returned from Korea after about a year of Army service there, called on his grandmother, Mrs. Lillie B. Coolidge a few days ago. Cpl. Coolidge, who was wounded in Korea last April, was returned to the front lines after several weeks of hospital treatment and spent about ten weeks with his regiment fighting on the high rocky hills of Heartbreak Ridge. At the end of his furlough in March, Cpl. Coolidge is to go to Fort Devens for reassignment to duty.

(This photograph is of Calvin, his mother Doris, his grandmother Lillie, and his father Franklin, taken on February 24, 1952, and found amongst the artifacts. At this time, Lillie lived at 11 Coolidge Drive. The farm was named "The Sego Sago," by Harry Coolidge. Sego Sago is an old Indian saying that means, "Welcome and Good Cheer.")

HEADQUARTERS
ALASKAN AIR COMMAND
APO 942, c/o PM, SEATTLE, WASHINGTON

AAPMP 510

28 February 1952

SUBJECT: Travel Authorization of Dependents to Alaska

TO: Commanding Generals,
First Army, Governor's Island, NY
Fifth Army, Chicago, Illinois
Sixth Army, Presidio of San Francisco, Calif
Seattle Port of Embarkation, Seattle, Wash
Chief of Transportation

1. The following named individuals, dependents of the personnel indicated who proceeded to the Alaskan Air Command pursuant to competent orders on a permanent change of station, are authorized to proceed from the places indicated, to which they proceeded under Career Compensation Act, 1949 to indicated Air Force bases in Alaska by commercial means and/or privately owned automobile. Travel by government air or government water is not authorized.

Name and address of dependents	Individual upon whom dependent (Sponsor)
Mrs Lela M. Young, Wife, 31 Janet C. Young, Daughter, 13 Doris G. Young, Daughter, 10 1268 Riverdale St, West Springfield, Mass.	S/Sgt Kenneth R. Young, AF 44038129 Hq Sq, 39th Air Depot Wg, Elmendorf AFB, Als TDN 5723500 248-341 P533.5 02 03 07 S99-999
Mrs Lenora R. Ruiz, Wife, 25 Steven L. Ruiz, Son, 5 Daniel M. Ruiz, Son, 2 336 Beach 54th St, Arverne, LI, NY	T/Sgt Louis M. Ruiz, AF 39283243 2107th Air Weather Gp, Elmendorf AFB, Als TDN 5723500 248-341 P533.5 02 03 07 S99-999 HHLD EFF: Trans Off, Great Falls AFB, Mont
✓Mrs Ann Soland, Wife, 23 1501 Riverdale St, W. Springfield, Mass	S/Sgt Norman J. Soland, AF 17198609 Flt "D", 10th Air Rsq Sq, Ladd AFB, Als TDN 5723500 248-341 P533.5 02 03 07 S99-999
Mrs Janice M. Mika, Wife, 28 312 Cottage Ct, Champaign, Ill HHLD EFF: Same address & agent	Capt Joseph F. Mika, AO 551893 1931st AACS Sq, Elmendorf AFB, Als TDN 5723500 248-341 P533.5 02 03 07 S99-999
Mrs Barbara A. White, Wife, 29 Judith A. White, Daughter, 1 19457 Andover, Detroit 3, Mich HHLD EFF: Frank Peter, Same address	S/Sgt William White, AF 19109665 5005th Hospital Gp, Elmendorf AFB, Als TDN 5723500 248-341 P533.5 02 03 07 S99-999
Mrs Kathryn C. Leighty, Wife, 24 Michael J. Leighty, Son, 6 328 13th St, Huntington Beach, Cal HHLD EFF: Maude Kramer, 705 Walnut, Huntington Beach, California	1/Lt Robert J. Leighty, AF 1587403 Hq Sq, 39th Air Depot Wg, Elmendorf AFB, Als TDN 5723500 248-341 P533.5 02 03 07 S99-999
Mrs Jacquelyn L. Jaques, Wife, 27 2216 S. Beverly Glen Blvd, Los Angles 64, Calif HHLD EFF: Agt- Wife, Same address, Loc-Great Falls AFB, Montana	Major Louis Jaques Jr, AO 372868 6th Radar Cal Flt, Elmendorf AFB, Als TDN 5723500 248-341 P533.5 02 03 07 S99-999

(These three pages consist of the "Application for Transportation of Household Goods," dated February 28, 1952. This is the paperwork Norman and Ann had to fill out in order to "transport" Ann to Fairbanks. Norman went first, by boat, but Ann traveled by plane seven weeks later. For those seven weeks, Ann stayed with Norman's aunt, Emilia Guttebo, in Seattle, patiently waiting for Norman to find the two of them a place to live.)

AAPMP 510 -2- (Cont'd)
28 February 1952

Mrs Laura M. Martin, Wife, 33	T/Sgt Harry C. Martin, AF 20455476
Sandra J. Martin, Daughter, 9	Flt "B", 10th Air Rsq Sq, Elmendorf AFB, Als
Judy C. Martin, Daughter, 7	TDN 5723500 248-341 P533.5 02 03 07 S99-999
Harry C. Martin Jr, Son, 2	149 Homja, San Bruno, Calif

2. Reimbursement for transportation will not exceed cost of travel from designated address to the continental United States port of embarkation servicing the Alaskan Air Command, and from the Port of Whittier, Alaska to indicated Air Force bases in Alaska.

3. Travel will not commence until immunizations listed in paragraph 4 below have been secured and arrangements have been made with the Army and/or Air Force installation designated for the shipment of household goods, if desired.

4. It is requested that the Commanding Generals, Army Areas indicated, upon receipt of these orders, designate a post, camp, or station which the dependent may contact to arrange for administering of the following immunizations and the shipment of household goods.

Small Pox Diphtheria Tpheid-paratyphoid Tetanus

5. a. Shipment of hoasehold goods and hold baggage to destination is authorized. Provisions of SR 55-160-1, AFR 75-33, dated 22 June 1949, and Chapter 8, Joint Travel Regualtions, dated 22 December 1950 apply.

b. Authority is granted for shipment of a privately owned automobile from a port of embarkation to a port of debarkation in the Alaskan Theater, by a military vessel. Delivery of the automobile to the port of embarkation is the responsibility of the owner and will be accomplished at the owner's expense.

6. Dependents will have mail addressed to them in care of the member of the service upon whom they are dependent, using the address of such member.

FOR THE COMMANDING GENERAL:

COBURN G. ARLEDGE
Captain USAF
Asst Air Adj General

DISTRIBUTION:
- Individuals copies THRU: First Army (75)
- Individuals copies THRU: Fifth Army (50)
- Individuals copies THRU: Sixth Army (75)
- TAG, DA Attn: AGAO-CT, Wash 25, DC (2)
- Hq, USAF, Wash 25, DC (2)
- C/T, Mvmt Con Div, Pers Mvmts Br, Rm 2924, Bldg T-7, Gravelly Point, Va (2)
- CG, SEPE, Seattle, Wash (2)
- Sponsors copies, each (2)

W

STANDARD FORM 116
AUGUST, 1949
PROMULGATED BY
EXECUTIVE ORDER 10053

APPLICATION FOR TRANSPORTATION OF HOUSEHOLD GOODS

(SEE INSTRUCTIONS ON REVERSE SIDE ITEMS 1 THRU 24 TO BE COMPLETED BY APPLICANT)

1. SHIP OR STATION: Ladd AFB, Alaska
2. DATE: 28th Feb. 52
3. SHIPMENT NO. *(No. of shipments to show sequence)*: 1

4. FROM *(Last name - First name - Middle initial)*: Soland Norman J.
5. GRADE, RANK OR RATING: S/Sgt.
6. SERVICE SERIAL NO.:
7. STATE TEMPORARY OR PERMANENT CHANGE OF STATION: Permanent

8. TO *(Submit to nearest shipping officer)*: Westover AFB, Mass

9. IT IS REQUESTED THAT ACTION BE TAKEN TO HAVE HOUSEHOLD GOODS TRANSPORTED AS PROVIDED BY LAW AND REGULATIONS BASED ON CHANGE OF STATION ORDERS ISSUED BY AT
UNDER DATE OF PARAGRAPH NUMBER ORDERS NUMBER
WHICH ORDERED ME TO DUTY AT

10. TO BE SHIPPED FROM *(Street address)*: 1501 Riverdale St. CITY OR TOWN: West Springfield DATE INSPECTION MAY BE MADE
11. TELEPHONE NO.: Spfld. 3-3625

12. TO BE SHIPPED TO *(Street address)* CITY OR TOWN DESIGNATED AGENT TO RECEIVE PROPERTY AT DESTINATION

13. APPROXIMATE AMOUNT TO BE SHIPPED
A. NO. OF POUNDS OR ROOMS
B. APPROXIMATE WT. OF PROFESSIONAL BOOKS, PAPERS & EQUIPMENT INCLUDED
C. SHIPMENT INCLUDES *(Check)* ☐ WASHING MACHINE ☐ REFRIGERATOR ☐ PIANO ☐ OTHER *(Specify)*
D. NO. OF BARRELS OF CHINA

14. METHOD OF SHIPMENT REQUESTED *(Check one)* ☑ AS DESIGNATED BY SHIPPING OFFICER ☐ RAIL, ☐ VAN, ☐ EXPRESS, OR ☐ AIR REGARDLESS OF SHIPPING OFFICER'S DESIGNATION
15. DATE BAGGAGE TO BE PICKED UP
16. OFFICIAL HOME

CERTIFICATIONS

17. I CERTIFY THAT THE ABOVE REQUESTED SHIPMENT CONSISTS OF HOUSEHOLD GOODS WHICH BELONG TO ME AND HAS BEEN IN USE BY MYSELF *(or family)* PREVIOUS TO DATE OF THIS REQUEST AND IS NOT INTENDED DIRECTLY OR INDIRECTLY FOR ANY OTHER PERSON OR PERSONS OR FOR SALE.

18. I FURTHER CERTIFY THAT THE ABOVE MENTIONED PROFESSIONAL BOOKS, PAPERS, AND EQUIPMENT, ARE IN FACT PROFESSIONAL BOOKS, PAPERS, AND EQUIPMENT WHICH ARE NECESSARY IN THE PERFORMANCE OF MY OFFICIAL DUTIES.

19. I WILL ACCEPT THE METHOD OF SHIPMENT DESIGNATED BY THE SHIPPING OFFICER TO BEST SERVE THE INTERESTS OF THE UNITED STATES AND MYSELF, OR WILL PAY ANY EXCESS COSTS OCCASIONED BY MY SELECTION OF ANY OTHER METHOD.

20. I WILL PAY ALL HANDLING, STORAGE, OR OTHER COSTS, NOT AUTHORIZED BY REGULATIONS.

21. IF MY ORDERS ARE MODIFIED OR CANCELLED AND AFFECT THIS SHIPMENT, I WILL NOTIFY IMMEDIATELY SHIPPING OFFICERS AT POINT OF ORIGIN *(or port if any)*, AND DESTINATION.

22. IN THE EVENT OF FAILURE ON THE PART OF MYSELF OR MY AGENT TO FURNISH THE SHIPPING OFFICER AT DESTINATION WITH PROMPT REMOVAL INSTRUCTIONS, I HEREBY AUTHORIZE THE ABOVE SHIPMENT TO BE PLACED IN LOCAL COMMERCIAL STORAGE IN MY NAME AND FOR MY ACCOUNT AND RISK.

23. UPON RECEIPT OF STATEMENT(S) SHOWING EXCESS COSTS I WILL REMIT AN AMOUNT SUFFICIENT TO COVER SUCH COSTS, OR PERMIT THE APPLICATION OF SO MUCH OF MY PAY AS MAY BE NECESSARY TO COVER SUCH COSTS. THIS AGREEMENT IS MADE WITH THE UNDERSTANDING THAT IT DOES NOT PREJUDICE MY RIGHT OF APPEAL TO THE COMPTROLLER GENERAL AND THE COURTS OF ADJUDICATION AFTER SUCH PAYMENT OR DEDUCTION HAS BEEN MADE IF I CONSIDER THE AMOUNT THEREOF TO BE ERRONEOUS.

24. PREVIOUS SHIPMENTS UNDER IDENTICAL ORDERS *(If none, indicate "None")*

FROM (A)	TO (B)	BILL OF LADING, CONTRACT OR PURCHASE ORDER NUMBER *(If known)* (C)	POUNDS HOUSEHOLD GOODS UNPACKED (D)	POUNDS HOUSEHOLD GOODS PACKED (E)	POUNDS PROFESSIONAL BOOKS, PAPERS, & EQUIPMENT (F)
None					

SIGNATURE OF APPLICANT: Mrs. Ann N. Soland

25. CERTIFICATE IN LIEU OF SIGNATURE ON THIS FORM IS REQUIRED WHEN REGULATIONS SO AUTHORIZE:
(To be accomplished only by the Commanding Officer or his authorized representative, by signature or official seal)

THE PROPERTY IS PERSONAL BAGGAGE, HOUSEHOLD GOODS, OR PROFESSIONAL BOOKS, PAPERS, AND EQUIPMENT AUTHORIZED TO BE SHIPPED AT GOVERNMENT EXPENSE.

REASON FOR NONAVAILABILITY OF SIGNATURE
NECESSITY FOR SHIPMENT
CERTIFIED BY *(Signature and Title)*

26. CERTIFICATE OF SHIPPING OFFICER

DESIGNATED METHOD OF SHIPMENT
BILL OF LADING NUMBER
METHOD OF SHIPMENT USED
CONTRACT NUMBER
EXCESS COST OF PACKING, CRATING, AND HAULING *(When required by the service concerned)* ☐ GOVERNMENT ☐ COMMERCIAL $
PURCHASE ORDER NUMBER
POUNDS HOUSEHOLD GOODS
POUNDS PROFESSIONAL BOOKS, PAPERS, AND EQUIPMENT
SIGNATURE OF SHIPPING OFFICER

STANDARD FORM 116

[Alaska was purchased by the United States for $7.2 million (about two cents an acre) from Russia in 1867 but it did not receive U. S. statehood until January 3, 1959. So, Norman and Ann lived in Alaska prior to it being an official state.]

(Fort Custer - FortWiki Historic U.S. and Canadian Forts.)

Letters from Calvin to his Parents
Cpl. John C. Coolidge
US51095649 C Btry.
711th AAA Gun Bn.
Ft. Custer, Michigan

April 5, 1952

Dear Folks,

Well I have finally been permanently stationed at Ft Custer in Battle Creek Michigan. *[Fort Custer was named after General Custer who was a native of Michigan.]*

Left Ft Sheridan Wednesday & arrived at Ft. Custer the same day. It is only about 180 miles east of Chicago.

I am in the 711th AAA outfit. It is an outfit that is used in defense against airplanes in principal cities. Right now the outfit is set up in Detroit, Michigan. They will be back Mon. and then will leave again Thurs. for some Camp in Wisconsin to do some firing.

I am going on sick call Mon. and get an appointment with a nose doctor to see about getting my nose fixed. So I am going to try and get out of going with the outfit to Wisconsin because they will be gone for three weeks and I want to get my nose fixed as soon as possible. Will be getting discharged sometime in June. Sure hope Uncle Sam comes through with that $45 a month bonus for combat veterans in Korea. I think I would get about $450. Boy!! I could use that when I get out.

Well not much news. I am okay, the cars okay, and I hope you are both feeling fine and not working to hard. Have you heard from Ann lately? I have got to write her.

The weather has been stormy & cold. It started snowing Thurs morning and it is still snowing. Will close for now. Write when you can

Love
'Cal'

PS. Did you get the money order ok.

(Fort Custer barracks, Battle Creek, Michigan.)

15 April '52

Dear Folks,

Received your letter dated April 10th yesterday and was glad to hear that everything was OK.

Was sorry I didn't have Norm's sisters address because I was in Detroit over the weekend and could have seen her.

Went to the hockey game Sun. night and saw Detroit & Montreal play in the third game of the Stanley Cup playoffs. Detroit won 3-0.

Jimmy Campbell from New York City went with me. He took basic with me at Devens. We went over seas together. Was in the same company in Korea. Rotated the same time, and here we are in the same outfit here. We will probably get discharged together to. Just 72 days to go.

I have an appointment the 23rd of this month to see a nose doctor. I probably won't get my nose fixed until sometime in May.

Well there is not much news. Still not doing much of anything here.

In Norm's letter he said something about wanting to buy the Ford. I'll write and tell him that he'll have to talk with you about that. Hope you both had a good Easter. Did you buy a new 'bonnet.' It rained all day Sunday in Detroit. Thank you for the swell card.

Love
'Cal'

April 24, 1952
[Calvin's birthday]

Dear Mom & Dad,

Received your letter and birthday card yesterday. That was a swell card. I can't believe yet that I am 26 years old. I suppose you can't either.

Those boys that rode out with me from home all went to different camps.

Haven't been going out much since I've been hear [here]. Plenty of good places to go to though but am running close on money. Either go to a show or down to the N.C.O. Club for a couple of beers.

There's a fellow in the outfit from Ohio who comes from a big family. He used to farm before he came into the Army.

He's a swell fellow. Has a terrific sense of humor. So we get along swell. He and I and Jimmy Campbell usually chum around together. He gets out in August.

Well there's not much news and I've got to write quite a few letters so will close for now.

Love
'Cal'

P.S. Got to give the Car a 5000 mile check up soon speedometer reads about 4300 miles now. Will write again soon. Got a letter from Johnny Colburn yesterday.

(This book of matches with photograph reads, "Remember your blind date?? Glad I met you." Signed, "Joan")

[This book of matches was found amongst the artifacts in the Coolidge home. As you can see in the photo on the left, Calvin is wearing his uniform and appears to be enjoying a bottle of beer with his blind date.]

May 7, '52

Dear Mom & Dad,

Received your letter of April 30th and was shocked and saddened to hear that Harriett Simpson had past away. Boy, Frank sure has got a job on his hands now. I sent him a sympathy card. It's still hard to believe because I had seen her at the party over to Eddie's just before I came out here. I remember you saying though that her blood pressure was high.

I haven't had my nose fixed yet but I am quite sure I will before I get out. I will be getting it fixed at Perry Jones Vets, Hosp. in Battle Creek. That's supposed to be quite a famous hosp. They have quite a few Korean Vets there now and a big list of operations to be performed ahead of mine but they are going to squeeze me in when the chance comes up. I guess they are going to break it and reset it. It will take about an hour to perform the operation. I'll be in the hospital about 10 days.

Not much news. Hope you are both in good health

Love

Cal

P.S. Battle Creek has two big cereal factories here, Kellogg & Post. Have you got Frank Caroleo's address?

May 29, '52

Dear Folks,

Have just come back from a ball game in Detroit. Our outfit has a bus and they take a bunch of guys to a game when they can. We get in for nothing. Saw the Detroit Tigers play the Cleveland Indians. Cleveland won 11-4. Had seats in the right field stands. Pat Mullen of Detroit & Simpson of Cleveland each hit homers. The batters came with the bases loaded and was caught by a guy who sat next to me. He caught it with his bare hands and hurt one of his fingers.

No I haven't got my nose fixed and it doesn't look like I will unless I stay in the Army longer. They have so many wounded coming there at Perry Jones and so few doctors that they have a list a mile long. I sure would like to get it fixed. I asked the doctor if it would get worse and he said no.

Things sure don't look good in Korea. In fact they don't look good in Europe either.

Well I'll be getting out soon and I don't know what I'm going to do. I would love to go to Alaska but I don't know if I could afford to at this time. If they pass the bill giving all service men who went over seas $300 mustering out pay I would go up. The paper said it would be passed by July or August. I could sure use it. Ann wants me to come up. Got a letter from her two or three weeks ago and they both seem to be doing good.

Aunt Ellen has written a couple of times and I guess she and Grandma would like to have me work the farm. With fishing allowed in boats now at the Quabbin a few cabins built up on the farm would do all right. [articles on pages 170 and 171] With Korean Vets getting the G.I. bill of rights I could go to school and get $110.00 a month. I would have to work part time if I did go to school. Well I have got to decide what I am going to do and what I want to do darn soon. I hate the thought of going back to work in the shop.

Well we get paid Sat. and I will send the money order then. I must have the suit just about paid for. Well I have got to write Ann and Norm so we'll close for now?

Love 'Cal'

("Welcome to Kellogg's of Battle Creek" postcard amongst the artifacts.)

THE BOSTON SUNDAY GLOBE—APRIL 20, 1952 A—5

Opening Quabbin "Greatest Thing That Could Happen to Fishing in This State"

By EARL BANNER

Fishermen's boats will be allowed on mighty Quabbin Reservoir for the first time in history next week-end.

This rapid follow-up by the Metropolitan District Commission on Gov. Dever's surprise announcement of a week ago may very well astonish members of the State Fish and Game Board, officials of the Division of Fisheries and Game, and some veteran employees of the Metropolitan District Commission itself who always have been and probably still are opposed to the move.

Metropolitan District Commissioner Edgar F. Copell told the Globe yesterday:

"We're still faced with a Herculean task, but the Commission will meet this Thursday to begin ironing out the details. Some of the questions we'll have to decide are:

★ ★ ★

Will outboard motors be allowed?

What will the hours of fishing be?

Shall we make a charge for a daily fishing permit and, if so, how much will it be?

★ ★ ★

But you can announce that fishermen with boats of their own will be allowed to put them in the water at Quabbin next weekend."

The establishment of a state operated boat rental livery and the promulgation of a completely brand new set of rules and regulations governing the public usage of the Quabbin area will follow "during the next few weeks," Mr. Copell said.

Anglers have been allowed to fish from the shores of Quabbin Reservoir at a few sites selected mainly for their inaccessability ever since 1946.

★ ★ ★

An M. D. C. official quite frankly told the Globe: "We selected these spots with inconvenience in mind. You have to walk several miles to get to most of them and 'patronage' hasn't been very heavy."

★ ★ ★

The Governor's announcement in Worcester a week ago that the big reservoir would be opened to boat fishing came as a complete surprise to most M. D. C. officials. Their first reactions are best described as "mixed."

It was pointed out by some that while the "public health angle" was no longer a valid argument against opening Quabbin to boat fishing (there are many precedents for using public water supplies as public boating and fishing areas in the west and nearby New York state), there was still the matter of "protecting the watershed from fire," "the business of regulating the fishery," "financing," etc. etc.

[illegible] a few hours [illegible] Mr.

(AP Photo)

[illegible] RESERVOIR, [illegible] domestic water supply reservoir in the world.d. The hand-

fishermen short, to my way of thinking."

Stroud believes that a self-perpetuating lake trout and walleye big game fishery can be established in Quabbin in as little as three of four years.

Meanwhile, while anglers wait for should be able to enjoy some of the the first year of what should be excellent big-game fishing, they best black bass fishing in Quabbin that they have ever known.

"Quabbin," Stroud contends, "is large enough to support year-round fishing of black bass, both large mouths and small mouths."

"Spring fishing for black bass is more exciting than the best trout fishing," Stroud believes. "Inch for inch and pound for pound, the smallmouth bass is the gamest fish that swims," he said.

Whether or not anglers will be allowed to fish for black bass on Quabbin this year before the nominal July 1 season opening date is just another one of the many, many problems that must be ironed out now by the M. D. C. and the Division of Fisheries and Game.

THE SPRINGFIELD SUNDAY REPUBLICAN, SPRINGFIELD,

Quabbin Reservoir Ideal Trip

Quabbin Reservoir is a scenic attraction for the motorist as well as a drawing card for boat fishermen.

By taking the road off Route 9 in Belchertown and driving past the administration building of the Massachusetts District Commission, motorists can view much of the reservoir. From the tower most of the 88.6 square miles can be seen. The reservoir impounds the run-off from 86 square miles of Swift River Watershed and has a shore line of 118 miles. Sixty islands dot the surface.

Four towns, Enfield, Dana, Greenwich and Prescott were discontinued and inundated to make way for the water supply. Persons living in 650 houses in the area were required to find new homes and 7561 bodies buried in 34 cemeteries in the area were removed to the present Quabbin Park Cemetery in Ware.

Fishermen can use this construction wonder and enjoy the scenic grandeur of the area while taking fish. Boat and shore fishermen are certainly getting a break. Through several gates, fishermen can walk to Quabbin's shore through shade-covered roads observe bird, animal and plant life of the preserve. No picnicking areas are provided and only fishermen are allowed.

(The article above, "Quabbin Reservoir Ideal Trip," published in The Springfield Sunday Republican, dated June 1, 1952, reads, "**Quabbin Reservoir is a scenic attraction for the motorist as well as a drawing card for boat fishermen.** By taking the road off Route 9 in Belchertown and driving past the administration building of the Massachusetts District Commission, motorists can view much of the reservoir. From the tower most of the 88.6 square miles can be seen. The reservoir impounds the run-off from 86 square miles of Swift River Watershed and has a shore line of 118 miles. Sixty islands dot the surface. Four towns, Enfield, Dana, Greenwich and Prescott were discontinued and inundated to make way for the water supply. Persons living in 650 houses in the area were required to find new homes and 7561 bodies buried in 34 cemeteries in the area were removed to the present Quabbin Park Cemetery in Ware. Fishermen can use this construction wonder and enjoy the scenic grandeur of the area while taking fish. Boat and shore fishermen are certainly getting a break. Through several gates, fishermen can walk to Quabbin's shore through shade-covered roads [and] observe [the] bird, animal and plant life of the preserve. No picnicking areas are provided and only fishermen are allowed.")

June 8, 1952

Dear Folks,

I have just come from fishing and thought I would drop you a few lines and am enclosing a $25.00 money order for the car. Was glad to hear that I got some money back on the insurance.

Have been going fishing quite often. They have some beautiful lakes hear [here] in Michigan. Have some good lakes right here on the post. It cost $1.00 for a license. Catch perch, bass, and bluegill mostly. Go with a couple of fellows who have all the fishing equipment including a boat. We have a swell time and it don't cost a cent. Cook the fish here at the company mess hall.

Glad to have gotten Frank's address. It looks like he will have to spend a full two years in the Army. He may be better off putting in a full two years. I only wish I was getting that mustering out pay when I get out. I guess they won't pass it until latter on this summer.

Well I guess I'll close for now. Got to do some washing. They have a washing machine here in our barracks so it don't take to long. You and Dad take it easy now and get out as much as you can.

Love Cal

P.S. Do I owe any more on the suit?

June 28, 1952

Dear Folks,

Well I should start my processing to get discharged next week. I think when I get out that I will stop at New York City and see some of the boys I was with in basic and overseas. I would like to take in a ball game or two. Would like to see the Giants play. I might stop in and see Norm's sister & husband in Detroit to.

Boy!! The weather here is hot. You don't feel like doing anything. Except going fishing that is. Will go fishing this afternoon and tomorrow.

How does Grandpa Clark feel now. It must be wicked laid up in bed [in] this kind of weather. I guess it's been awful hot back home to. Read in the paper where it was 105 in New York.

Been playing some softball every Sat. evening with the battery. We play other batteries and are doing pretty good.

I hope that G.I. bill comes through for Korean Vets soon. We will get $300 mustering out pay. Will also get loan and school benefits.

How's the fishing up at the reservoir. I bet there [they're] catching big ones. Have you been up to the farm lately? Many blueberries?

Will you see you all soon Love

Cal

*[The envelope is postmarked **July 17, 1952**, but there is no date on the following letter. The back of the envelope is dated too, but with the "Rec'd" date of July 18, 1952.]*

Battery "C"
711th AAA Gun Battalion
Fort Custer, Michigan

Dear Folks,

No, I haven't left 'Custer' yet. I have started processing for discharge and expect to finish in about a week.

I have been transferred to the 5010 ASU here at Ft Custer. It is a rotation and discharge center.

The 711th was discharging men but it has gone back to Alabama. So they sent me along with some other fellows who are due for discharge over to the 5010.

Because of the close transfer I've been held up for two weeks. The way they operate around here is a shame. Of course the Army is still paying me.

I am sending $55.00 money order for the car. I have got the car in ship shape. Changed the tires around last night.

I'll be getting about $220.00 when I get discharged. That includes transportation. You have to wait about a week before you can pick up your money at Finance here

If nobody rides home with me I'll come straight home and will not stop at New York City.

Hope everybodies OK

Love

'Cal'

(ABOVE: This photo was taken May 31, 1953, of a picnic held behind Ann and Norman's house with friends in Alaska. Norman is sitting second and Ann, third. BELOW: Norman is leaning on his truck in front of their trailer where they lived until he was able to build them a house in front. They then lived in the house and rented out the trailer.)

Letters from Ronald to Doris and Franklin

N3C Ronald W. Bein – A.F. 11204727
6101 ST Installations Sqdn.
A.P.O. c/o P.M. San Francisco, Cal

24 Nov. '52

Dear Aunt Doris & Uncle Frank,

Received your letter today and was pleased to hear from you. Hope that you are all fine. I am feeling pretty good but have had a tiring weekend. Worked all day Saturday and Sunday driving a truck. Hope to get a day off sometime this week. Today it is raining and I have been working in the office, catching up on some paper work that was about a month behind. Glad to hear that Ann & Norm have a house, but I imagine it is rather a miserable task hauling their water.

Well, this will be my second Christmas away from home, and that is the time when I really get homesick. When I hear "White Christmas" and "Blue Christmas" on the Juke Box at our Club, it really gets me. I go to our club practically every night. Usually take my girl and dance a little. They play Bingo there every Wednesday night, and this last week I won $32.50. I have been pretty lucky and I really did need the money too. Well, I'm expecting my C.O. to pay me a visit here this afternoon, so I had better close for now and clean the place up. Say Hello to "Cal" for me. Hope to hear from you again soon.

Love,
Ron [Bein]

29 Dec '52

Dear Aunt Doris & Uncle Frank,

Received your Christmas card and gift and was very pleased. Hope that you folks had a nice Holiday. Our club burned to the ground about a week before Christmas, and our plans for a party went up with it. Had a few partys in our shops day before Christmas, but I didn't do any drinking. As a matter of fact, I expected to get loaded, but in the end I was sober as a judge. Probably was the best thing anyway.

Received a card from Ann & Norm which was very nice. Grandpa Clark's death shocked me. I had a long talk with him when I was home on furlough and he was tickled to have me stop in to see him. Guess he was quite lonely in the past years. Well, I have lots of letters to write, so if you'll excuse me, I'll close for now.

Hope to hear from you again soon. Thanks again for the lovely card and gift.

Love,
Ron [Bein]

1953

...and thereafter

[The following letter is from Norman's mother and father, Luise and Embret Soland, written to Doris and Franklin Coolidge, Calvin and Ann's parents. Luise and Embret Soland are in the photo below.]

Decorah Iowa
Jan-22-1953

Dear Folks–

Happy New Year to you all, hope you folks are all well, we are all well. There is a lot of flu, all around us but so far we have escaped having it. We had a letter from Norm & Ann with some pictures taken, during the Christmas Holly days. [Five photos follow.] We sure enjoyed them, it was so much fun seeing there [their] new house & how nice they have everything inside. Norm is so proud of Ann, she is a good housekeeper.

Maybe you folks will take a trip to Alaska when the new arrival comes! We have a little baby boy in The Soland family, they came home for xmas so we could see him, there [they're] so nice when there so little. It will also be fun to have Norman & Ann come home but it will be so far for them.

There really isn't much news. I wanted to write a few lines along with those pictures. The weather here today is foggy & may rain as it's so mild. Hope we'll have snow instead.

Wishing you folks the Best of Luck through the coming year.

Respectfully, Mr. and Mrs. Soland

(These five photos were taken the week of Dec. 15, 1952. ABOVE: "LADD AIR FORCE BASE – AMERICA'S FARTHEST NORTH AIR BASE." BELOW: A pregnant Ann, working in the kitchen.)

(ABOVE: The plane Norman used to fly rescue missions with Air Rescue. BELOW: Norman, Ann, and the couple who rented their trailer after Norman built the house—Barb and Doug.)

(ABOVE: Ann and Norman enjoying a meal. BELOW: Telegram dated February 20, 1953, from Ann and Norman Soland to Doris and Franklin Coolidge regarding the birth of their first child, Linda Dianne Soland.)

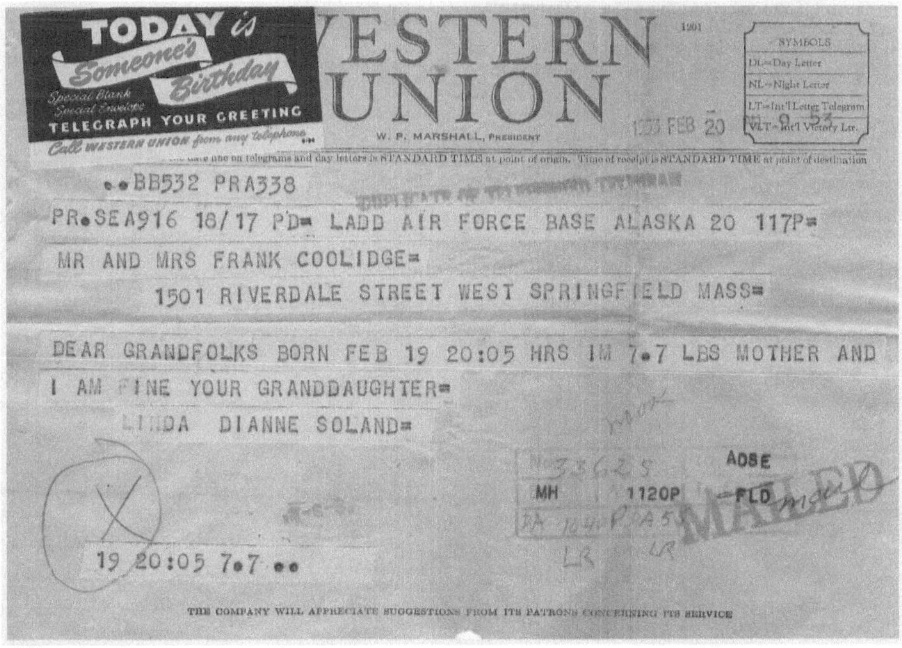

TODAY is Someone's Birthday
Special Blank Special Envelope
TELEGRAPH YOUR GREETING
Call WESTERN UNION from any telephone

WESTERN UNION

W. P. MARSHALL, PRESIDENT

SYMBOLS
DL=Day Letter
NL=Night Letter
LT=Int'l Letter Telegram
VLT=Int'l Victory Ltr.

1953 FEB 20

..BB532 PRA338

PR.SEA916 18/17 PD= LADD AIR FORCE BASE ALASKA 20 117P=

MR AND MRS FRANK COOLIDGE=

1501 RIVERDALE STREET WEST SPRINGFIELD MASS=

DEAR GRANDFOLKS BORN FEB 19 20:05 HRS IM 7.7 LBS MOTHER AND I AM FINE YOUR GRANDDAUGHTER=

LINDA DIANNE SOLAND=

ADSE

MH 1120P FLD

MAILED

19 20:05 7.7 ..

THE COMPANY WILL APPRECIATE SUGGESTIONS FROM ITS PATRONS CONCERNING ITS SERVICE

KILLED IN ACTION

HENRY S. TENCZAR

WEST SIDE GI DIES IN KOREA

Henry S. Tenczar Killed in Action, Parents Informed

Mr. and Mrs. Frank Tenczar of 1158 Piper Rd., West Springfield, have been notified by Army authorities, of the death of their son, Henry S. Tenczar, in action in Korea. Henry would have been 22 April 1. No other information was given.

A graduate of West Springfield High School class of 1950, he entered military service August 20, 1952, assigned to the 7th Infantry.

Only recently letters were received

Continued On Page 10

West Side GI

Continued From Page 1

by his mother and sisters, dated March 16, in which he said he was fine, everything was alright and told his mother not to worry. He said he expected to return to Japan that week.

Besides his parents, he leaves three sisters, Mrs. Millie Podolak and Mrs. Julia Gargalanski of West Springfield and Mrs. Rose Ashe of Springfield; and three brothers, Edward, Philip and Theodore, at home. Henry was a member of Holy Family Parish, Brightside.

"West Side GI Dies in Korea," Henry S. Tenczar killed in action. Henry was a friend of Calvin's.

Letter from Ann to her Parents
May 5, 1952 [she meant 1953]

Dear Grandma,

I am sending along a little gift for “Mother’s Day.” My mami picked it out, but I like bright colors. I am 10 weeks old now and weigh 13 lbs. My casts have been off for 2 wks. and my feet look pretty good. I have 8 dresses and my mami is going to make me one if Daddy buys her sewing machine. Don’t tell her, but I think Daddy will get her one for “Mother’s Day.”

Mami took me shopping this afternoon and I’m tired & fussy, so I will be a good girl and sleep for Mami. “Happy Mother’s Day.”

Lots of hugs & kisses,
Little Linda

P.S. The picture enclosed was taken on Easter Sunday. I am laughing.

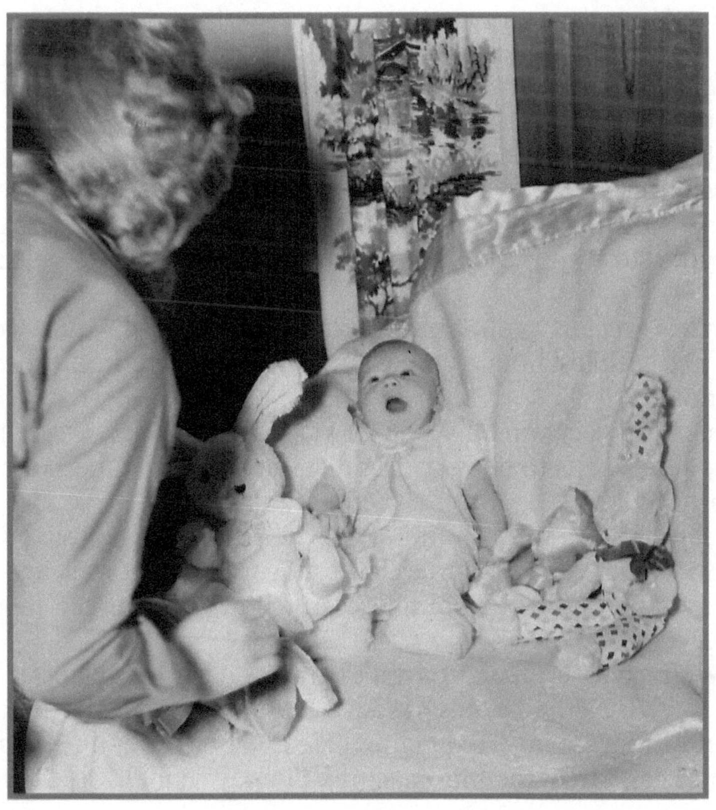

[The following letter was enclosed in the same envelope as the previous one from "Little Linda."]

Dear Mom,

Wish we could buy you more, but I know you like scarves. We sent one to Norm's mother with the green border.

Have been trying to get my spring cleaning done. Norm washed all the windows, inside & outside. The curtains you sent me look real nice. I took down the drapes & curtains on the door & put them (the ones you sent) up. They brighten up the room & let in the sunshine. I hung them at midnite last nite. The only time I can get anything done is when Linda is sleeping. Yesterday I gave the floor a good scrubbing & this morning I wiped over it & polished it. Also made 2 pie shells yesterday A.M. & made one a banana cream.

This afternoon I drove Barb and Theresa into Fairbanks & went to the PX & Commissary on the Base. So I am pretty tired. Linda is nursing right now. Is she chunky, but solid. My Sears order arrive today. I got a pretty yellow plastic shower curtain with big swans on it. Also material to match from which I'm going to make curtains for the bathroom. There are two windows in the bathroom. Tomorrow afternoon I have to wash clothes. Theresa is going to come with me and watch Linda. The last time I washed I was up 'til 1 A.M. Linda was fussy. Her tooth bothered her, I guess. Don't get much sleep anymore. But she's pretty good during the day. Sleeps 4 hrs. at a time, but she likes to stay awake in the evening 'til about 10:00 or 11:00 P.M.

Norm is on alert again tomorrow nite and Thursday nite we're invited to a couples' house for dinner. I'm going over in the afternoon with Linda.

It has been very warm. We just have the furnace on low at nite. The sun here seems to be very bright & warm. We get it on our side in the afternoon.

I meant to have told you that Peggy & Ralph (the couple I said would try & visit you sometime) left for Worchester 2 wks. ago tonite. Anyway, Ralph put in our plumbing. And Norm scrounged most of the pipe.

How's Foxy Grandpa? I haven't heard you say much about him lately. How's the stand doing? Wish I could've seen Cal in the Minstrel. [Program inserted below.] He must have changed since I saw him. I can't imagine him teaching Sunday school.

You know, we never sent Grandma & Aunt Ellen any gifts yet, but as soon as we get a few extra pennies we'll do so. I hate to go shopping now, as I have to take Linda when I go.

Every one thinks Linda is a beautiful baby. She wants to sit up all the time now. She thinks "gooing" is cute, I guess, & will keep it up for hours. We took her to the movies the other nite. She sat in my lap watching the objects change on the screen.

Guess I'll close. Norm will be here soon.

Love,
Ann, Norm, & Linda

Did Trombley come to see you?

(This photo was used for Ann and Norman's 1953 Christmas card, here posing with Linda, their first child. Ann made Linda's coat.)

THE MINSTRELS OF THE

GENERAL ELECTRIC ATHLETIC ASSOCIATION

PRESENT

FROLICS OF 1953

H. B. Lawrence School --- Holyoke, Mass.

April 12, 13, 14

(The following are pages from the "Frolics of 1953" program dated April 12, 13, 14, 1953. There is a total of four pages.)

Welcome to the

" Frolics of 1953 "

presented by the

Minstrels of the General Electric Athletic Association

Directed by .... ROBERT J. WHITTAKER

Interlocutor .... JOHN McCORMACK

Pianist .... ETHEL ROCHE WELLER

Tickets .... BOB McCUTCHEON, CLAIRE BOISSONEAULT

Programs .... WALTER MALEC, JAMES O'CONNOR

Ushers .... BERTHA AND JOAN MURPHY

Music by .... JERRY LAMOTH'S ORCHESTRA

H. B. LAWRENCE SCHOOL
April 12, 13 and 14, 1953

We would like to thank the cast, and everyone who in any way contributed to the success of this show. We are grateful to the contributors to this program and respectfully solicit your patronage of their products.

THE MINSTREL COMMITTEE,
Frederick L. Cassidy,
General Chairman.

Because of the length of our show, we request that no encores be asked for.

—PROGRAM—

PART I

1. *Opening Chorus* . . . . The Entire Company

2. End Song: "*Tuck Me to Sleep*" . . . . Art Higgins

3. Specialty: *Accordion Solo* . . . . Joseph Kielec, Jr.

4. Solo: "*I Wish I Had My Old Girl Back Again*" Ed. Lally

5. Specialty: *Dance Routine* . . . . . . Pupils of Elsie Cappel

6. End Song: "*Put Your Arms Around Me Honey*" Fred Cassidy

7. Solo: "*Wonderful Copenhagen*" . . . . . . Jules Silverstein

8. Specialty: "*Recitation*" . . . . Robert Branflick

9. End Song: "*Oh! You Beautiful Doll*" . . . . Roger Curtin

10. Solo: "*Keep It a Secret*" . . . . John Cooledge

11. Specialty: *Song* . . . . Donna Marie Boissonneault

12. End Song: "*No Help Wanted*" . . . . . . Maureen Morgan

13. Solo: "*Have You Heard*" . . . . Margie Miller

— INTERMISSION —

During Intermission the following will take place:

Specialty: *Imitations* . . . . Claire Boissoneault
Specialty: "*The Auction Modern*" . . Nick Sarro, Bud Sardam

(Calvin is listed in the program as "John Cooledge.")

—PROGRAM—

PART II

1. Opening Chorus: .... The Entire Company
2. End Song: *"They Go Wild"* .... Bob Smith
3. Solo: *"Tell Me You're Mine"* .... Everett Burke
4. Specialty: *Dance* .... Joseph Cassidy of (Lally School of the Dance)
5. End Song: *"Rock-a-Bye Your Baby"* .... Howie Moran
6. Solo: *"Because You're Mine"* .... Gloria Roy
7. Specialty: *Song Stylist* .... Jim O'Connor
8. End Song: *"Ida"* .... Don Hebert
9. Specialty: *Dance Routine* ...... Pupils of Elsie Cappel
10. Solo: *"The Desert Song"* .... Ted Musgrove
11. Specialty: *"The Ballet Extraordinaire"*
12. Solo: *"There Are Such Things"* .. Archie Archambault
13. End Song: *"Birth of the Blues"* .... John Kelly
14. Closing Chorus .... The Entire Company

Midnight Sun

Farthest North Service Newspaper in the World

LADD AIR FORCE BASE, ALASKA

VOLUME I, NUMBER 15 — 1 — JULY 1, 1953

Top 3 Grades Promotion List is New Feature

... a special feature each ...omotion month, the Midnight ...n will publish the first three grade promotions for the entire Ladd AFB. Lower grade promotions could be carried except for the amount of space that it would take to print them. The following is a complete listing of Army and Air Force promotions for the month of June.

(Continued on Page 8)

S BULLETIN ★

f the Associated Press and the
Midnight Sun)

dio promptly and coldly rejected the
nistice now on terms already agreed

wer's special emissary to South Korea
persisted in his refusal to accept the

★ ★ ★

erman Officers were being recalled
e questioned as to why the Soviet
t revolt of several thousand German

★ ★ ★

Representatives today agreed to spend
the coming fiscal year.

★ ★ ★

(D-Ga.) made his formal argument
Court Justice William O. Douglas,
committee promptly told him he had

ediately after Douglas had issued a
he full court, to hold off the electro-
Ethel Rosenberg.

★ ★ ★

nd Dependents authorized to purchase
ck up a new PX card as soon as
will be made without the new pass.

★ ★ ★

he Fourth of July will bring Nome
in the seacoast city. A full turnout
group of military personnel from
full day of activities.

★ ★ ★

all units to call the Sun Office, 31102,
Give your outfit a hand and help

Nome Celebrates 4th As . . .

Ladd Units Journey North

The City of Nome, Alaska, and the troops stationed there will see the greatest celebration ever held at the seacoast city. Units from Ladd will fly to Nome for the 4th of July to take part in a full day program.

Actually the 4th of July celebration will start Friday evening with four Ladd softball teams playing two games under the "midnight sun" at the City Airfield.

Saturday, the 4th, the activities will start at 10 a.m. with two hours of children's sports. From noon to 1 p.m. ice cream and C-rations will be given out to the kids by Army personnel from Ladd. From 1 to 1:30 a drill exhibition will be held and from 1:30 until 2 there will be a parade of all marching units from the city of Nome and the military units. The 774th Air Force band will play for the parade.

At 2 in the afternoon patriotic services will be held with an invocation and an address by Mayor Steve Anderson. Guest speaker for the day will be Lt. Col. Harold A. Williams, Commander, 5003rd AB Sq. Nome.

At 2:30 Eskimo sports will be the feature attraction and at 4 p.m. team sports such as a tug-of-war, a pillow fight and relay races.

Retreat will be sounded at 5 and at 5:30 a skeet shoot will be held.

The evening will be topped off with an American Legion Dance, a roller skating exhibition, and Eskimo dances.

Personnel from Ladd include 2 flights of Air Force enlisted men and two plattons from the Army. One officer and four Air Policemen will handle the ceremonies. Four softball teams and the 774th Air Force Band will also make the trip.

Project Officer for the day will be Major Lester Hunt.

New PX Passes Now Being Issued

Military dependents and authorized civilian personnel must have the proper PX card after July 1 if they make purchases in the Ladd Post Exchanges.

Major John Klepper, PX Officer stated that the system now being used in the States will start here on July 1. He explained that military depndents and authorized civilians over the age of 16 years must bring their identification pass to the PX office in the Hospital Building to obtain a new PX pass.

The PX office is open from 8 to 5 weekdays and passes must be picked up during these hours.

Major Klepper reminds all personnel that the Post Exchange hours are from 11 to 6 on weekdays and from 9 till 4 on Saturdays.

74th Rescues Civilian Pilot

Guy Rivers, a local mine owner was rescued Sunday by a Coast and Geodetic Survey helicopter after being found by the 74th Air Rescue Squadron at Ladd. Rivers was forced down by engine trouble last Friday and was reported lost Sunday.

After 15 minutes in the search area Sunday morning his plane was spotted but he had left the plane.

Captain Grummel and 1st Lt. Moore tried to follow a river which the man was apparently travelling but lost him after spotting him on a sand bar.

A helicopter from Galena was brought to the scene where the man was found and a pick-up made. He was then flown by the Air Rescue Squadron to Ladd.

Mr. Rivers had walked about two days and had put only 15 miles behind him. He seemed well enough after his experience and upon reaching Ladd, stated he thought he could have made the 30 miles out of the woods without too much trouble.

Wellington, Kans., (AFPS)—Auto dealer Herb Etter would like to get his hands on a no good sidewinder who identified himself as Norman Good and purchased an automobile by signing his check "N. O. Good."

(An article on a rescue performed in part by Norman Soland in Alaska, published in the MIDNIGHT SUN "Farthest North Service Newspaper in the World," dated July 1, 1953. The title reads, "74th Rescues Civilian Pilot.")

Yes Honey, I Do . . .

Ladd Airman Weds Girl In ZI By Phone

Perhaps a bit out of the ordinary this month was the wedding of A/3C Alva Ford of the 5th Laison Detachment to his girl, Elizabeth Joye, in Greenville, South Carolina.

At a total cost of $33.00, which Airman Ford said was "well spent," he was married here at Ladd June 13th at 10 a.m. His wife, however, was married at 3 p.m. in Greenville, S. C.

According to Airman Ford, "We sent several letters back and forth getting the thing set up and then we put in a call. There was a minister and my girl on phones in her parents' home. They (her relatives) were listening in on other phones or a speaker or something and I had A/2C Garner Graham listen in from up here. The minister just married us like he would anyone else."

Within 24 hours his wife met him at the Fairbanks Airport to give him the first kiss of married life. She had boarded a plane just minutes after their conversation and departed for Fairbanks.

Airman Ford, who has only been in Alaska three months, said, "I couldn't get a leave to go get married and bring her up here, so that seemed to be the only way to do it."

"You asked me to drop in sometime!"

Auto

—Photo by Finan

PICTURED SHORTLY AFTER arriving at Ladd are the members of the 74th ARS who took part in the search last Sunday with Guy Rivers, the object of their search. Left to right are S/Sgt. Norman Soland, Captain Robert Grummel, Captain Frederick Bateman, A/2C Joe Hall, Mr. Guy Rivers, A/1C Robert Kenney, and Lt. William Mohr. All took part in the search activities.

[A letter was found dated July 11, 1953, that refers to this news article. It was from Ann "Coolidge" Soland, who was writing from Alaska, to "Grandma, Grandpa, & Uncle Cal." The letter reads, "Norm was on 'alert' last nite, and about 11 P.M. came home with a watermelon, 6 muskmelons, 6 native tomatoes, & 8 peaches. One of 74 Rescue's planes came in from Calif. last nite with all that stuff & the fellows divided it. Of course they had to pay for it. I ate a whole tomato, it tasted so good. And I made a bacon, lettuce, & tomato sand. I had melon for breakfast, and we had watermelon for supper. It was delicious.... I am also sending in another envelope the Ladd Base paper. Norm's picture is in it. Was taken after he had gone on a mission, looking for that Bush Pilot who cracked up his plane near Nome. He wouldn't have to go on so many missions if it wasn't for those darn (wanted to say damn) bush pilots. You may keep it."]

[The following is an article that was published in Life Magazine, dated June 14, 1954. A caption under one of the photos in the article reads, 'The Rescuers guide Argus' sled around an ice embankment on the way down Muldrow Glacier. Eight-man rescue team included Army buddies of Argus, who said, 'This looks like old home week.'" My father, Norman Soland, was one of those men on that rescue mission. Flying rescue missions was one of the things he did while serving his 20 years in the Air Force.]

ON MT. McKINLEY: RESCUE AFTER VICTORY

On April 17 four young men set out to climb Mt. McKinley in Alaska, one of the world's most formidable mountains. One, Elton Thayer who organized the expedition, was a park ranger. Another, Morton Wood, was a Fairbanks farmer. The others, Leslie Viereck and George Argus, were privates on Alaskan duty. All were experienced mountain climbers, excited at the chance of challenging the 20,269-foot-high peak. Mt. McKinley, highest point on the North American continent, soars farther (over three miles) from its base than even Mt. Everest, which rises from a 16,000-foot-high plateau. Northernmost of the world's great peaks, it is enshrouded nearly all year by poor weather, and only a half-dozen parties have reached the summit since 1913, when climbers first achieved it.

To make their task even more impressive, the Thayer party set out to reach the summit over the southern approach, which no one had ever been able to do before. First they climb to the basin of Ruth Glacier at 5,000 feet, where Wood's wife, piloting a plane, air-dropped them fresh supplies. Ascending the glacier, they crossed the strip appropriately named Very Narrow Ridge. At the foot of an ice slope they were immobilized for three days by a heavy snowstorm. When that stopped it took four more days to hack out 1,038 steps needed to negotiate the ice slope. Then after climbing a terrifying series of ridges, they had to drop down 2,000 feet and go up again on another tack, constantly imperiled by ice avalanches and impeded by sheer walls of ice.

Finally, on May 15, they moved out of their high camp at the 17,000 foot level and by midafternoon reached the peak. They stayed there for half an hour before starting down. Then tragedy overtook the Thayer party in this high blue-and-white world of sky and snow.

The story of the climb, disaster and the harrowing events which followed is told on the next four pages in photographs taken by the climbers themselves and a rescuer. Throughout the expedition Les Viereck and Morton Wood took superb pictures in both color and black and white. Dr. John McCall of the University of Alaska, who headed the rescue operation, took pictures of that effort. All of these add up to memorable documentation of the story of endurance, achievement, death and rescue.

After probably leaving their names and the date in a tin can at the summit, the four climbers started the descent, stopping overnight at 17,000 feet. Maneuvering down Harper Glacier and Karstens Ridge, the going was relatively smooth until they came to a steep, dangerous ice slope. Argus started gingerly across, Wood, Viereck and Thayer following. Midway, Thayer lost his footing and all four men, tied together, tumbled 1,000 feet down. Thayer broke his back against an ice outcrop and died instantly. Argus severely dislocated his hip. The other two, though badly shaken, were intact.

For a week the three survivors camped in a tent on Muldrow Glacier slope, hoping Argus would get well enough to move. He did not, and Wood and Viereck made a tough decision. They shifted Argus to a safer spot nearby and put the available food, a week's supply of oatmeal, powdered eggs and chocolate, within his reach. Then they left him in the howling loneliness of the glacier and started down for help.

Wood and Viereck started down Muldrow Glacier on Sunday, May 23, [1954] then cut through a pass to a ranger hut at Wonder Lake. They reached it Tuesday but found no one. Pushing on six miles to a prospector's cabin at Kantishna, they met rangers searching for the overdue climbers. A rescue party was standing by at Fairbanks, headed by Great Glaciologist John McCall. A helicopter dropped them onto Muldrow Glacier and then, flying above safe altitude, kept landing supplies farther up as McCall's party fought toward Angus' tent in the snow and over the treacherous ice.

In his lonely tent Argus kept busy sketching the mountains he could see, trying to read his one book—Mark Twain's short stories—and listening to the relentless, maddening fall of ice on nearby slopes. His hopes waned and he seriously considered making crude crutches and trying to hobble down the mountain. Then, after seven days and seven nights, he heard a voice yell, "Are you O.K.?" And he poked his head out of the tent to shout a heartening "Sure I am" to his rescuers.

THE SPRINGFIELD DAILY NEWS, SPRINGFIELD, MASS., WEDNESDAY, OCTOBER 31, 1956

PVA Awards Go to Best Hampden County Roadside Stands

The Pioneer Valley Assn. has made awards to Hampden County winners in the annual roadside stand competition for registered operators. Bluebird Acres at 736 Parker St., East Longmeadow, took the top award. Left: Gene Wiezbicki, operator, receives a plaque from County Commissioner William Stapleton, center, as PVA President Homer C. Perkins, right, looks on. Right: Second award went to Valley Farms at 1492 Riverdale St., West Springfield. Mr. Perkins, left, makes presentation to Cal Coolidge, operator of the West Side agricultural center. Judges examined all stands registered in the contest before selecting Messrs. Wiezbicki and Coolidge as the outstanding exhibitors.

(This was an article in The Springfield Daily News, dated October 31, 1956. On the far right is Calvin's father, Franklin, who is receiving the PVA award for "Best Hampden County Roadside Stands," on Calvin's behalf.)

(Calvin is standing in front of the VALLEY FARMS vegetable and fruit stand, taken in November of 1956.)

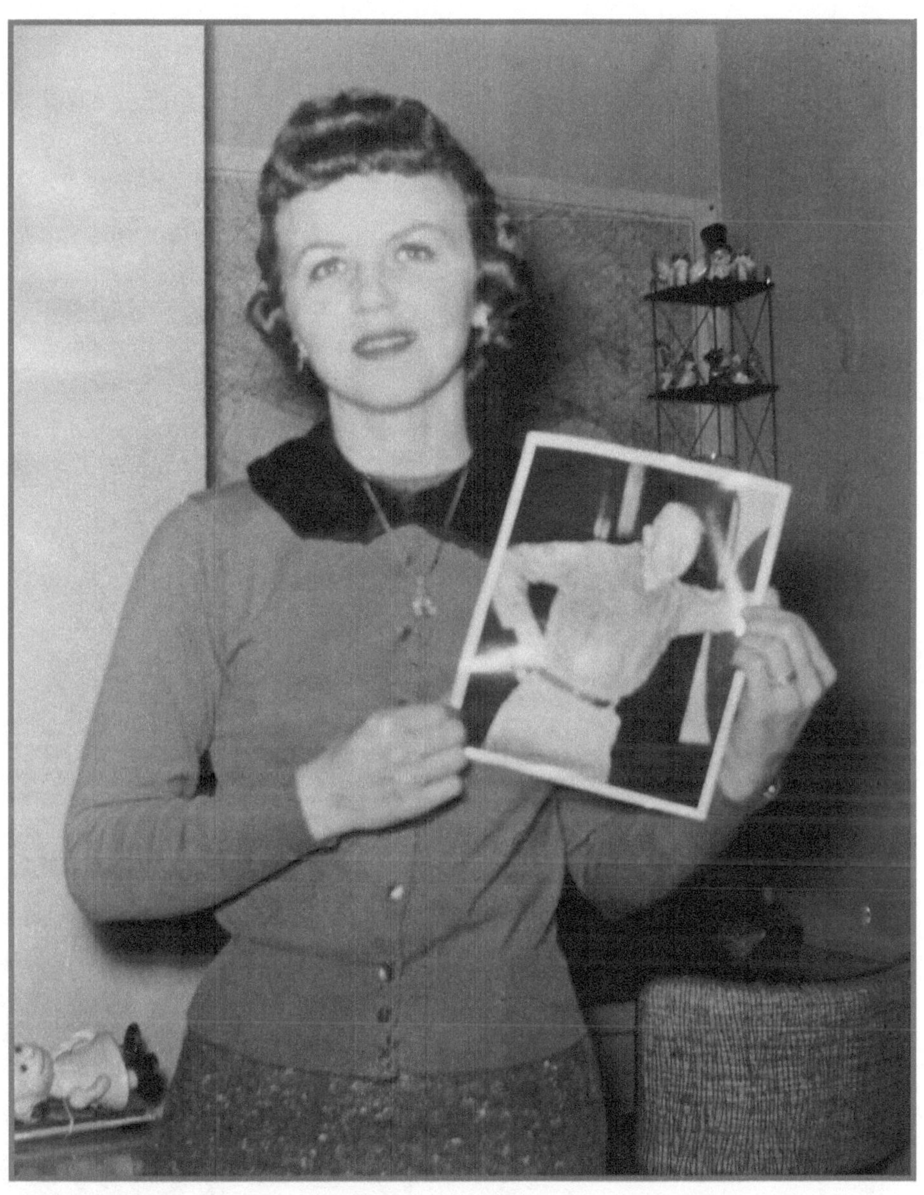

(In 1959, Ann "Coolidge" Soland lived in Decorah, Iowa, while her husband, Norman J. Soland, lived in a remote location in Alaska, continuing to serve in the Air Force.)

(Norman Soland worked in a remote site in Alaska for one year during 1959, while his wife, Ann, lived in a rented home in Decorah, Iowa, with their then five children. TOP LEFT PHOTO: Taken in April of 1959. Bottom row: Gary, Trudy, Great grandmother Lillie, Linda, and Cindy. Top row: Doris, Franklin, Norman holding Kathy, Calvin, and Ann. BOTTOM LEFT PHOTO: Norman wrote on the photo's front right, "we live here," along with an arrow pointing to where he lived. On the photo's back he wrote, "can hardly see white bubbles on top of the mountain." ABOVE: Norman is standing by what he calls "our control panel.")

Letter from Norman to Doris and Franklin

[Norman is now a T/Sgt]
4 Aug. 1959
Tuesday 18:30

Dearest Frank Dores & Cal,

Have meant to write to you so often, & just to darn lazy I guess. In school I was short on time to even read my night assignments & week ends, well I wouldn't miss a day with my family for no one. We drove the ford 17000 miles in 16 weeks. Actually drove the wheels off it. Between home & Chicago it ran from 4:20 to 4:55 would leave home at 01:30 Chicago time & be there for coffee & school. I never got the ford Wide open, Better sense I guess. But did hold 80 - 85 & quite often on each trip would run over 100 for a short spurt. knowing the car, checking it at both places on a hoist, I never worried about the car, only some thing or some one on the road. As it was I never had any real close calls & was quite lucky. We had awful rough going on our trip from Mass. Hit snow In Chicago, & had it from there on. We got some nice movies, when you get out have Ann show them, if she can find them. [*Norm is referring to home movies they took of their trip.*] From the Iowa border to home took us three days. Little over 100 miles. Going thru school on leave before & afterwards I was always thinking of this lop eared year & now that I'm counting the days, Well I just feel better about it. Your Daughter, my Wife, is really some woman, no need to explain. I told her I would quit if she wanted me too, But she said no, & deep down I felt like it, & often wonder if she didn't want it too. But wonderful her would not be the one to say. Sure hope we won't be sorry. Needless to say, I do worry about her, & I can't do much except count these endless days & hope time will leap a whole year in one fast jump. Maybe you can do me a favor, & I would be grateful. Write to her often & be awfully cheerful, she worries about you all, working as hard as you do. Believe if you wrote her, it would be a big help. She is busy with the kids, can't figure out, if its better with 5 small children, or if there were none. But they must be company for her, & that should be an asset. Also Frank try to spend Christmas with them. thats so important, as I know time will be endless then for her. I told her I would fly down, but now that I've seen the situation, daught [doubt] if its at all possible. Don't tell her, will wait awhile. I called her from Seattle before taking off, & she was perty well broken up, then I called her from Anchorage twice. The last time she was her wonderful self, & believe all is fine. I have had 2 letters from her in 3 weeks But I know it is because of mail situations here. We have 3 mail calls a week because of our location. It cost $500 for the mail plane each trip, & that [is] the reason. She has plenty [of] room so you could stay all winter if you could do it. But the main time would be Christmas. Sure didn't take me long, once I found the right girl, & she is sure Queen all the way.

I'll give you a run down on our job here. I'm going to be up near McGrath Alaska NW of Anchorage. Right now I'm at Middleton Island down in the Gulf of Alaska, the island is 4 miles by 3/4 & is about the same set up as mine will be. I'm here for school, & not very satisfied with it. We have plenty of work ahead of us. Lots of 12 hour days, 7 day weeks, the way it looks. As you know we generate electricity for the whole camp with diesels. I'll be with the 717 AC & W Sqdn. that stands for Air Craft Control & Warning. Our Generators & engines or [are] 100 KW rated that means it will supply 100,000 Watts or light 1000, 100 Watt bulbs per engine. We have 10 engines so we could, with no strain light 10,000 of those. this will give you an idea as to how much power my plant puts out—total 1,000,000 watts of electricity. Cal, imagine a plane flying with 5 minutes of fuel & in an emergency, fire, engine trouble—etc, then put him in a storm. Normally he's in no sweet [sweat]. G.C.A. (Ground Control Approach) will guide him thru the mountain passes & unto the runway—fine—But if one of my engines quite [quit] Radar is gone, if it goes that plane & crew is gone. So if this should happen, I'll be a S/sgt when I see you all next summer. If it happens twice, an A/ic. No matter come 70° below or what may, that engine will run, or automatic bust. It's a little like a game of poker only I don't like the stakes. that is why we have 10 engines. We run 4 all the time, 24 hours a day, with 4 standing by & 2 to work on & maintain. Now if one should grunt, grown, or smoke, or even look like its tired, we take it off & put a good one on. the stand by's are not guesses, they must be ready to take a 100 KW load right now, if needed. Believe me, I like a job wear daught [doubt] is not possible, but I don't like the consequences. I've told Ann I don't fool with electricity at all, don't say any thing else to her. the power house I'll have up north cost about $700,000 & they are really nice. the engine alone isn't as big as the 600 KW's we went to school on. They are about 7' high & 12-14 feet long. About the size of your car. We seem to think they will do a good job tho & unless we get in some bag [bad] fuel oil aren't bad at all. Cant get any more paper into one envelope. So I'll go up this way. *[Norman writes up the right side of the piece of paper, back up to the top where there is some room.]* Sure should like to hear from you all, but would rather you write to Ann. I'll write more later & tell you more about this jail sentence I've got. Take care of your selfs & don't over work.

Love,
Norm

(Norman wrote on the back of this photo, “this is 5 of 11 engines.”)

(Photo taken on Warren Air Force Base, Cheyenne, Wyoming. Top row: Ann "Coolidge" Soland holding Kathy, with Norman on the right. Bottom row: Linda, Gary, Cindy, and Trudy.)

Mrs. Lillie Coolidge

NEW SALEM – Mrs. Lillie (Pierce) Coolidge, 89, of Coolidge Drive, North New Salem, died late last night at Franklin County Public Hospital.

She was taken there by Orange town ambulance Sunday noon. She was the widow of Harry Lyman Coolidge, who died in 1948.

The family came to New Salem from Prescott in 1918. Mrs. Coolidge was born in Prescott, Sept. 18, 1873, daughter of Daniel T. and Ellen A. (Peirce) Pierce.

She was a founder and historian for the Prescott Historical Society. At the age of 70 Mrs. Coolidge published aa book "Past Events of Prescott." She was Orange Townsend Club Secretary.

She leaves a son, Franklin Pierce Coolidge, of West Springfield; a daughter, Miss Ellen A. Coolidge of North New Salem, with whom she lived; two grandchildren [Calvin Coolidge and Ann "Coolidge" Soland], six great grand-children [Linda, Trudy, Gary, Cindy, Kathy, and Lisa Soland, children of Ann and Norman Soland.] and several nieces and nephews.

Funeral services will be Wednesday afternoon at 2 at Higgins Funeral Home, Orange. Rev. Lydia Wood of Templeton will officiate and burial will be in South Cemetery, Orange.

There will be no calling hours.

A TRIBUTE
published in the pages of
THE RECORDER GAZETTE
GREENFIELD, MASS.

DEC 18 1962

Memorial Obituary

Mrs. Lillie Coolidge

NEW SALEM — Mrs. Lillie (Pierce) Coolidge, 89, of Coolidge Drive, North New Salem, died late last night at Franklin County Public Hospital.

She was taken there by Orange town ambulance Sunday noon. She was the widow of Harry Lyman Coolidge, who died in 1948.

The family came to New Salem from Prescott in 1918. Mrs. Coolidge was born in Prescott, Sept. 18, 1873, daughter of Daniel T. and Ellen A. (Peirce) Pierce.

She was a founder and historian for the Prescott Historical Society. At the age of 70 Mrs. Coolidge published a book "Past Events of Prescott". She was Orange Townsend Club secretary.

She leaves a son, Franklin Pierce Coolidge, of West Springfield; a daughter, Miss Ellen A. Coolidge of North New Salem, with whom she lived; two gand-children, six great grand - children and several nieces and nephews.

Funeral services will be Wednesday afternoon at 2 at Higgins Funeral Home, Orange. Rev. Lydia Wood of Templeton will officiate and burial will be in South Cemetery, Orange.

There will be no calling hours.

(ABOVE: Obituary for Lillie Pierce Coolidge, who died December 18, 1962. Her husband, Harry Lyman Coolidge died November 30, 1944. Their son, Franklin Pierce Coolidge, died December 9, 1968, and Franklin's sister, Ellen Adeline Coolidge died in 1984. Franklin's wife Doris Elizabeth "Nesbit" Coolidge died at 101 years old on August 16, 2009. Lillie wrote a book entitled *Past Events of Prescott, Mass.*, which was published in 1949 by Roy W. French of Orange Enterprise and Journal Publishing.)

(As stated in Lillie Coolidge's obituary, these are her six great-grandchildren. The youngest and seventh, Bryan, was born later. Back row: Trudy, Linda holding Lisa the editor of this book, and Gary. Front row: Cindy and Kathy. This photo was taken in front of their home on Warren Air Force Base in Cheyenne, Wyoming.)

(Calvin Coolidge's wife, Christy "Arendt" Coolidge, taken in 1977 for Antioch High School in Antioch, Illinois, where she taught for 28 of her 30 total teaching years.)

(ABOVE: Photo taken at Calvin and Christy's wedding, August 11, 1975, in her aunt's cabin in Land O' Lakes, Wisconsin. Norman Soland was Calvin's best man. From left to right: Doris Coolidge, Calvin and his wife Christy, and Christy's mother, Charlotte Ruby Pauline "Wincentsen" Arendt. BELOW: Calvin and Christy at Antioch High School's Prom, May 17, 1980. Christy wrote to Doris, her mother-in-law, on June 13, 1980, "Enclosed find a picture of Cal & I taken at Prom. Doesn't he look snappy in his tuxedo.")

(ABOVE: Calvin Coolidge with his niece Lisa Soland in March of 1999 following a performance of The Swing Sisters, who were headlining at the Ramada Express Hotel in Laughlin, Nevada. Calvin and Christy drove from their home in Arizona to see the show. BELOW: J. Calvin Coolidge is standing in front of his fruit and vegetable stand located at the end of the driveway of the Coolidge home on 11 Coolidge Drive in New Salem, Massachusetts. People drove from miles around to purchase Cal's produce, particularly his remarkable tomatoes.)

(This photo was taken in the living room of the Coolidge home at 11 Coolidge Drive in New Salem, Massachusetts, at Doris Coolidge's 100th birthday celebration, on August 25, 2007. Doris' actual birthday was on August 29th. Sitting on the couch: Norman Soland and his wife Ann, Doris Coolidge, Calvin Coolidge and his wife Christy, Lisa Soland and her husband, Deryk Stilwell. Back row: Bryan Soland and his sister Cindy Soland. Doris sat where she is seen here for much of the party while her friends passed through the room wishing her a wonderful birthday. At one point, Doris replied, "All my friends have gotten so old.")

(ABOVE: Ann and Norman riding in Ogden Pioneer Days' Grande Parade, which runs through the heart of Ogden City, July 24, 2012. Norman was honored for his participation in the Berlin Airlift of 1948." BELOW: This photo is of Norman and Ann Soland on December 28, 2021, while celebrating their 70th Wedding Anniversary in the Veterans' home where Norman lives.)

Welcome to the memorial page for
John Calvin Coolidge
April 24, 1926 ~ October 13, 2016 (age 90)

John C. Coolidge

NEW SALEM- John Calvin Coolidge passed away at home in New Salem on October 13, 2016 from cancer.

He was born in Athol on April 24, 1926 the son of Franklin Pierce Coolidge and Doris Nesbit. He grew up in West Springfield and began farming there at a very young age.

He served in the army during the Korean War and received a Purple Heart when he was wounded at the Battle of Heartbreak Hill.

In 1975, he married Christy Arendt in Land O' Lakes, Wisconsin. He worked for his brother-in-law, Norman, who owned a landscaping company in Spring Grove, Illinois until he returned to Massachusetts where he resumed farming. He has been growing and selling vegetables at Coolidge Farm in New Salem for over 25 years.

He is survived by his wife of 41 years, Christy; a sister, Ann (Norman) Soland; five nieces, Linda (Jeff) Sterbenz, Trudy Soland, Cindy Bergh, Kathy (Robert) Titchbourne, Lisa (Deryk) Stilwell; and two nephews, Gary (Jody) Soland and Bryan Soland.

There are no calling hours.

A celebration of life party will be held in April at the Coolidge Farm.

Witty's Funeral Home, 158 South Main Street, Orange, is directing the arrangements.

[Note: Calvin was not wounded "at the Battle of Heartbreak Hill," as this memorial page states. Though he fought in that battle, he was actually injured on Hill 902 in the Battle of King's Hill. The Stars and Stripes article depicting this battle can be found on page 93.]

(A postcard of President J. Calvin Coolidge with this family was discovered amongst the artifacts.)

[Below is an article from The Watertown paper, dated July 3, 1930, about the descendants of John and Mary Coolidge, who came to the United States in 1630. I have typed the article to make reading it more accessible, but when I carefully unfolded the newspaper, it crumbled into pieces at the crease, so there were a few words I had trouble reading.]

THE WATERTOWN
A COMMUNITY NEWSPAPER

Watertown, Massachusetts, Thursday, July 3, 1930

"Coolidge Clan" gathers in annual reunion on the old Watertown Home...

More than 200 descendants of John and Mary Coolidge, the colonists who came to Massachusetts Bay in 1630, with Governor Winthrop and Sir Richard Saltonstall, assembled at Watertown last Saturday to hold their annual reunion in the town where their ancestors settled. This was the 24th meeting of the members of the family, the first one having been held, strangely, just fifty years ago this summer. Coolidges came from all over the United States to attend this meeting during the Tercentenary of Massachusetts Bay. Among them were men and women from Chicago, Ill., Rhode Island, Connecticut, Detroit, Mich., Plattsburgh and Syracuse, N. Y., Maine and New Hampshire, and many from distant cities and towns in Massachusetts.

They gathered at the old Coolidge homestead, 703 Mt. Auburn Street, where at about 12 noon they were greeted by members of the local branch of the family who had hospitably opened their home for their cousins. Several of these members were quite appropriately gowned in old colonial garb, with kerchief and lace cap; these being Mrs. Emma Coolidge Rugg, Mrs. Mattie Coolidge Crawford, Miss Elsie Coolidge, Mrs. Emily Coolidge Reid, and Miss Rosamond Coolidge.

During a most delightful social hour the guests visited, met new comers, and went to the old burying-ground to see the ancient stones that mark the graves of their ancestors, John and Mary Coolidge, and other members of the old generations, Lieut. Richard Coolidge, and Joseph Coolidge, to whom his descendants erected in 1875 a monument in memory of his death just one hundred years before, the only Watertown man to fall at the Battle of Lexington and Concord. They also enjoyed the old home, with its contents of other days, where Joshua Coolidge, born in 1796 erected his home, before this one was erected by the father of the host, Mr. Herbert.

Luncheon served in Tent

Luncheon was served in a large tent on the front lawn, and after luncheon, Mr. William Henry Coolidge, of Manchester, the president of the Coolidge Family Association, opened the business meeting with a welcome to all guests on this most noteworthy occasion. His dry bits of wit made the meeting most enjoyable. Mr. Herbert Coolidge had prepared a most interesting welcome as host, with history of his own family, which he was unable to give, and which was read most pleasingly by his daughter, Miss Delpha Coolidge. The president then introduced a member of each branch of the family, there being descendants of four sons and one daughter of John and Mary Coolidge, Mr. William Coolidge Lane spoke for the youngest branch, Jonathan; Doctor Algernon Coolidge, descendant of this same son, also brought a message; Mr. Joseph Austin Coolidge, of Cambridge, spoke wittily for the second branch, Simon; Dr. Charles Davenport, of Newton, spoke for the descendants of the one daughter, Mary; and Hon. Marcus Coolidge, of Fitchburg, as descendant of the third son, Nathaniel, spoke most amusingly of Will Rogers and democratic Coolidges. All gave much of interest or humor in their brief remarks.

The president called for report of progress as to consideration for a gift or memorial to the Parish of Cottenham, England, where John Coolidge was born, by the chairman, Mrs. Fred Crawford, and the Association voted that the president should appoint a committee to carry forward this excellent enterprise, in honor of their ancestor. The officers who were already serving the Association were unanimously re-elected; namely, Mr. William Henry Coolidge, of Manchester, president; Mr. Francis Lowell Coolidge, of Boston and Milton, vice president; and Miss Nettie E. Coolidge, of Framingham, secretary-treasurer.

Miss Emma D. Coolidge Speaker

The president then introduced the speaker of the afternoon, a descendant of the eldest son, Ensign John, Miss Emma Downing Coolidge of Newton, historian of the family and chairman of the Genealogical Committee. Miss Coolidge is an author, with many books to her credit, and she has just completed for the Association a Genealogy brought up to date as its share in the celebration of the Tercentenary, a book containing over 350 pages. She is the daughter of John Henry Coolidge, L.L.B. of Natick, lawyer and writer, and the grand-daughter of Col. Alexander Coolidge, selectman of Natick, Middlesex County coroner for forty years and commissioned lieutenant of cavalry in 1828 by Governor Levi Lincoln on whose staff he served. Miss Coolidge is a prominent clubwoman in Newton and Massachusetts, and her tercentenary poem, "Our Torch," she read as the closing of her speech.

The "Historical Address" contained many personal bits of history of descendants, as well as accounts of early generations. Miss Coolidge began with records of the family in England, where seven generations were recorded at Arrington and Cotam, with quaint wills, showing y [?] possessions, and the kindly, generous character of these people. She described the coat of arms, and turmoil, religious and political, between 1620 and 1630, which resulted in the coming of John and Mary Coolidge to Massachusetts Bay. She described the interesting character of John Coolidge, affectionately called "Goatman" [?] Coolidge and "Old Father" Coolidge, with the public offices he held, his inventories of estates and [?] of wills which proved him a man of education and legal attainment. She then took up by branches the outstanding figures of the years, which proved that all have been interested in the same field, law, writing, and politics. In each branch were found men who served well in the Revolutionary War, in the War of 1812, in the Civil War, and many were in the World War, some with the distinction of [?] guerre and other metals.

Men of outstanding military career in the branch of the eldest son began with Ensign John himself and his son, only 14 years of age, who served in King Philip's War. After Sherborn there was Major Isaac Coolidge, and Capt. John Coolidge, the [?] commissioned by Governor Francis Bernard in 1762, the French and Indian Wars. He removed to Natick and his four sons served in the Revolution; one, John, Jr., being left in the field at Bunker Hill, for dead, but who proved very much alive and was the only Coolidge to ride fifty years later to the laying of the cornerstone of Bunker Hill monument where Gen. Lafayette was the honored guest. Judges who descended in the line are Judge Edwin Morse and Judge Henry Coolidge Mulligan, of Natick. Judge Bruce of Malden, and one of Lawrence. Amongst prominent lawyers in this branch [?] Coolidge of [Natick]. His brother was Hon. Louis Arthur Coolidge, assistant secretary of the treasury under Pres. Roosevelt, and author of several notable books.

Other writers in this branch are Dane Coolidge, author of western stories, of California; Dr. Emelyn Lincoln Coolidge, famous baby specialist, whose articles appear in New York magazines; and Grace Coolidge Pennypacker, author of children's stories.

Many Famous Coolidges

For a descendant of the second son, Simon, Coolidge Corner was named. David Coolidge of Watertown married in 1814 Susan Griggs, of Brookline, and here he had a fine farm near what was later called Coolidge Corner, and two of his descendants had grocery stores at this corner, both of which facts gave the name to the location. A prominent judge, Judge Ashbel Gould Coolidge, of Rutland, Vt., and an educator, Prof. Guy Coolidge, of Wesleyan College, Kentucky, are descendants from this son. Three of the most distinguished men of the present day also spring from this son of John and Mary Coolidge; namely, ex-President Calvin Coolidge; Leigh Hill Coolidge, a naval architect of Seattle, Wash., whose models of diesel tugs are world-famous; and Dr. William David Coolidge, of the General Electric Co., Schenectady, N. Y., the greatest physical scientist of the age, who has had bestowed upon him every gold medal that organizations of world science can bestow.

Among descendants of the third son, Nathaniel, owner of the famous fishery weirs, there are three prominent judges: Hon. Frank Wesley Coolidge, of Redfield, S. D.; Judge Henry Hiel Coolidge, and Judge Orville William Coolidge, both of Michigan. There were also many Revolutionary soldiers and World War heroes, among them General Jonathan Coolidge of Waltham. Men prominent in politics, senators, and representatives include Hon. Frederick Spalding Coolidge, of Westminster, father of Hon. Marcus Coolidge, of Fitchburg, also well-known; Hon. Richard Coolidge, mayor of Medford; and all the Hoars, Senator Samuel; Hon. Ebenezer Rockwood, and Hon. George Frisbee Hoar. One noted family have the architect, David Hill Coolidge; his famous son, Frederick Shurtleff Coolidge, a surgeon; Albert Sprague Coolidge, at whose beautiful Pittsfield home are held annual musical festivals, and donor of the concert hall at the Library of Congress; and the most famous architect in the world today, Charles Allerton Coolidge, of Boston, who designed the Harvard Medical school and dormitories; Leland Stanford, Rockefeller Institute, Chicago Public Library, Art Museum and Law School, besides many beautiful buildings at Boston.

Descendants of the youngest son Jonathan, who was a surveyor and who surveyed the town line between Newton and Watertown, include many well-known diplomats and educators. Prof. Julian Lowell Coolidge, Prof. Archibald Cary Coolidge, and Dr. Algernon Coolidge are known as Harvard professors; Hon. Thomas Jefferson Coolidge was Minister to France and John Gardner Coolidge was Minister to Nicaragua. Joseph Randolph Coolidge, an architect of note; John Templeman Coolidge, famous landscape painter; Harold Jefferson Coolidge, well-known lawyer; Mayor Sidney Coolidge, a scientist of Harvard Observatory and with Commodore Perry's expedition to Japan; and the noted warrior Brig.-Gen. Charles Austin Coolidge, who served in the Civil War, Indian Campaign, Spanish War, Philippines and Boxer Uprising, we're descendants of this son of John and Mary Coolidge. This last name was a descendant of John Coolidge who married Lydia Dawes, sister of the famous William Dawes, rider with Paul Revere, and his record during the Revolutionary War in service of the patriot Joseph Warren is most interesting.

After the program the guests visited places of interest.

Herbert Coolidge Condenses the Family History

Ladies and Gentlemen of the Coolidge Family Association:

As I am the oldest living patriarch of the Watertown Branch of our Association, I have been asked to offer a few words of welcome from the Watertown members to those from the rest of the country. I do not propose to bore you with a long discourse on the virtues and vices or begets and begots of our line of descendants, but I should like to give you a short account of a few salient points with the idea that at subsequent meetings other lines of the family might follow my example, so that in the course of time we may acquire a symposium of interesting stories of those wonderful people–present company excepted, of course.

According to Bond's History, the first child of John Coolidge to be born in Watertown was a son named Simon. He was born in 1632. This Simon had a grandson of the same name, born in 1704, who was the father of the Joseph Coolidge killed in the battle of Lexington. The ancestral house which once stood nearby on Grove Street is said to have been built by one of these Simons, but we do not know which one. The tradition is that the house was already an old one when occupied by Joseph in 1775, so, whichever Simon was the builder, it is almost certain to have been the nesting-place of some of the forebears of the Honorable Calvin Coolidge. There were many others Simons in the other branches of the family, but I feel confident that it must have been one of these other branches that begot the immortal "Simple Simon."

Joseph Coolidge had two sons in their early teens, Joshua, 16, and Joseph, 14, who worked all night with their yoke of oxen and building the fortification on Bunker Hill. In the morning they were told that, inasmuch as they had worked all night, they might go home with their oxen and there hold themselves in readiness for a sudden call. They went home, but the battle occurred while they were on their way and they knew nothing about it until it was all over. That is how it came to pass that I am here to tell you the story, for our line descends from the elder brother Joshua.

The old Grove Street house was occupied by my grandfather, John Coolidge, for some twenty years from about 1820 to 1840, when the old gentleman moved to his palatial new house just across the street. The old house was then occupied by my father and I was the last Coolidge born in it in January, 1851.

The only thing concerning this last Coolidge born in the old house is that, although he is a very modest man he carries the greatest name of the Coolidge tribe. He is responsible for the names of two presidents of the United States–Herbert for Hoover and Coolidge for Calvin, but he must have been overlooked as he never secured a position in the Cabinet of either president.

Regrets Tearing Down of Old House

It is to be regretted that this old house was torn down. It might have escaped that fate if the Society for the Preservation of New England Antiquities had been organized earlier, but I am informed that the Watertown Historical Society will erect a recording-stone on the site.

There are interesting traditions of the old fellows who lived there. For instance, my great-grandfather, Joshua, was reputed to have hearing as keen as a fox. He had chopping-blocks in the yard of the dwelling. It is said that if he were away over the hill a half a mile distant, he could hear the boys cracking nuts on the chopping blocks, and would utter a mighty roar to the boys to desist because chips of nut-shells might injure the edges of the axes and hatchets.

The farm was a large one and employed a considerable number of men in the summer time, chiefly green Irishmen right over from the blogs of Ireland, or lumbermen from the north of New England. My grandfather's new house had a long ell with three large kitchens. The family kitchen was next to the main house and the second kitchen was for the laboring men. My grandfather, John Coolidge, was a deacon of the Baptist Church. It was his practice always to say Grace before meat; also when the men were gathered around the dinner-table it was the old gentleman's custom to carve the meat and see that every man was well served. He would then go forward and dine with the family in the main house. One day, when the men were gathered about the table, he saw the arm of the newly hired lumberman shoot out to the bread-plate. The old gentleman raised his hand, holding the carving knife, and said, "Hold on there, my friend. It is customary here to say a little something before beginning to eat." The man looked up with his mouth open and answered, "All right, Boss, go ahead, say anything you like, you can't turn my stomach."

It was the old man's habit to shave every night before going to bed. He used to draw a chair up to the kitchen-stove which he would use as a table and by the light of a little petticoat whale-oil lamp he would draw enough warm water from the tea-kettle to answer his purpose. One night a green Irishman who knew nobody and had nowhere to go, lounged in the kitchen and took pity on the old man sitting by the stove. He stepped forward, took the lamp in his hand and moved it around grandfather's face as he plied the razor from side to side. When the shaving was finished, the old gentleman said, "Thanks, Pat, but I suppose you noticed I had no mirror."

Joshua Coolidge Remarkable Man

Probably the most distinguished member of our Watertown branch was Joseph Coolidge, a grandson of the Joseph who was killed at the Battle of Lexington and a first cousin of my own father. Joshua was quite a remarkable man. Although a farmer, he acquired by himself the reading knowledge of French and German after he was fifty years of age. He was a great reader, having a large library of his own, and he was one of the founders of the Watertown Free Public Library. He also served in many important town offices. He was an earnest anti-slavery man and a friend of Wendell Phillips. A considerable musician, he played several instruments, and held the position of organist in the Baptist Church in Watertown. He was an intelligent and liberal-minded man. It is said that when the last hymn was sung, prior to the sermon, he would slip out of the church and run over to the neighboring Unitarian church to hear the eminent

Rev. John Weiss preach. He would then rush back to play the Doxology for the Baptist church. Among his descendants are a daughter and two granddaughters who are members of this association and who are with us today.

In my youth, Watertown was a beautiful town with neat farms and large estates with velvety lawns. It is now an imperial city of two-tenement dwellings, but I want to appeal to you to be loyal to your old stamping-ground and to the bones of your ancestors which rest in yonder cemetery. From the original John Coolidge down, our branch has been born, and lived and died in Watertown. I can find a record of only one man who moved out of town and he subsequently returned and died here.

We cordially welcome you to Watertown and trust you will have a very pleasant time. I am sorry we cannot offer you the cheer that this occasion demands, but the old decanter that used to stand on the sideboard, chiefly for the benefit of the minister, has been placed on the retired list—without a pension.

LARGEST CI ULATION IN WATERTOWN—NO FREE

THE WATE

A COMMUNIT

NINTH YEAR—No. 41 8 PAGE WATERTOWN, MASS., T

"COOLIDGE CLAN" GATHERS IN ANNUAL REUNION ON OLD WATERTOWN HOME

More than 200 descendants of John and Mary Coolidge, the colonists who came to Massachusetts Bay in 1630, with Governor Winthrop and Sir Richard Saltonstall, assembled at Watertown last Saturday to hold their annual reunion in the town where their ancestors settled. This was the 24th meeting of the members of the family, the first one having been held, strangely, just fifty years ago this summer. Coolidges came from all over the United States to attend this meeting during the Tercentenary of Massachusetts Bay. Among them were men and women from Chicago, Ill., Rhode Island, Connecticut, Detroit, Mich., Plattsburg and Syracuse, N. Y., Maine and New Hampshire, and many from distant cities and towns in Massachusetts.

They gathered at the old Coolidge homestead, 703 Mt. Auburn Street, where at about 12 noon they were greeted by members of the local branch of the family who had hospitably opened their home for their cousins. Several of these members were quite appropriately gowned in old colonial garb, with kerchief and lace cap; these being Mrs. Emma Coolidge Rugg, Mrs. Mattie Coolidge Crawford, Miss Elsie Coolidge, Mrs. Emily Coolidge Reid, and Miss Rosamond Coolidge.

During a most delightful social hour the guests visited, met new comers, and went to the old burying-ground to see the ancient stones that mark the graves of their ancestors, John and Mary Coolidge, and other members of the old generations, Lieut. Richard Coolidge, and Joseph Coolidge, to whom his descendants erected in 1875 a monument in memory of his death just one hundred years before, the only Watertown man to fall at the Battle of Lexington and Concord. They also enjoyed the old home, with its contents of other days, where Joshua Coolidge, born in 1796 erected his home, before this one was erected by the father of the host, Mr. Herbert Coolidge.

TALL

ge began
generations. Miss Co n England,
with records of the fami e recorded
where seven generation am, with
at Arrington and Cott y posses-
quaint wills, showing ious char-
sions, and the kindly, described
actor of those people. urmoil, re-
the coat of arms, and t een 1620
ligious and political. the coming
and 1630, which resulte to Massa-
of John and Mary Cool ed the in-
chusetts Bay. She des olidge, af-
teresting career of John an" Cool-
fectionately called "Go dge, with
idge and "Old Father his inven-
the public offices he of wills
tories of estates and education
which proved him a m hen took
and legal attainment. ng figures
up by branches the out that all
of the years, which ame field,
have been interested in In each
law, writing, and poli n served
branch were found me ar, in the
well in the Revolutionar War, and
War of 1812, in the Ci ar, some
many were in the Worl le guerre
with the distinction of cro
and other medals.
y career
Men of outstanding mil on began
in the branch of the eldes and his
with Ensign John hims o served
son, only 14 years of age Shorborn
in King Philip's War. dge, and
there was Major Isaac C ter com-
Capt. John Coolidge, the cis Ber-
missioned by Governor F d Indian
nard in 1762, the French and his
Wars. He removed to Nat volution;
four sons served in the the field
one, John, Jr., being left but who
at Bunker Hill, for dead was the
proved very much alive a ars later
only Coolidge to ride fifty stone of
to the laying of the corne Gen. La-
Bunker Hill monument whe t. Judg-
fayette was the honored gu line are
es who are descended in th Henry
Judge Edwin Morse and Judge
Coolidge Mulligan, of Judge one of
Bruce of Malden, an Natick; lawyers
Lawrence. Am Judge St ry Co
in this branch minent

CAMERA CLUB AT WATERTOWN

Front row (left to right) Murray Burbank, Ed Draper, Earl Holmes.

Middle row—Demeter Kollian, Eleanor Chase, Erwin Butterfield.

Back Row—Wilbur Woodland, Richard Davis,

Activities of the present day at the Senior High School are many and widely diversified so that each pupil may find a working group with a program which is of interest to him. Various clubs have been introduced during the past few years which have proved highly successful, and one of these which has made marked progress has been the Camera Club.

This club, under the guidance of Miss Helen A. with Edward Daniel Draper urer, and Murra ian, has enjoyed the most ence.

One of the club was the album of mailed to ulty, who is absence.

"40 & 8" BOYS HAVE REPAST AT EXPENSE OF SCHOOL BOARD

Two important functions were carried on at the Town Hall on Satur- d hereby hangs a tale. wreck" being put on

EAGLES D WATER BY 6

WATERT LEAGU

K. of C.
W. A. A.

(The original newspaper crumpled in the creases when it was opened.)

"COOLIDGE CLAN" GATHERS HERE IN ANNUAL REUNION

(Continued from Page 1)

vard professors; Hon. Thomas Jefferson Coolidge was Minister to France and John Gardner Coolidge was Minister to Nicaragua. Joseph Randolph Coolidge, an architect of note; John Templeman Coolidge, famous landscape painter; Harold Jefferson Coolidge, well-known lawyer; Major Sidney Coolidge, a scientist of Harvard Observatory and with Commodore Perry's expedition to Japan; and the noted warrior, Brig.-Gen. Charles Austin Coolidge, who served in the Civil War, Indian Campaign, Spanish War, Philippines and Boxer Uprising, were descendants of this son of John and Mary Coolidge. This last named was a descendant of John Coolidge who married Lydia Dawes, sister of the famous William Dawes, rider with Paul Revere, and his record during the Revolutionary War in service of the patriot Joseph Warren is most interesting.

After the program the guests visited places of interest.

Herbert Coolidge Condenses the Family History

Ladies and Gentlemen of the Coolidge Family Association:

As I am the oldest living patriarch of the Watertown Branch of our Association, I have been asked to offer a few words of welcome from the Watertown members to those from the rest of the country. I do not propose to bore you with a long discourse on the virtues and vices or begets and begots of our line of descendants, but I should like to give you a short account of a few salient points with the idea that at subsequent meetings other lines of the family might follow my example, so that in the course of time we may acquire a symposium of interesting stories of those wonderful people—present company excepted, of course.

According to Bond's History, the first child of John Coolidge to be born in Watertown was a son named Simon. He was born in 1632. This Simon had a grandson of the same name, born in 1704, who was the father of the Joseph Coolidge killed in the battle of Lexington. The ancestral house which once stood nearby on Grove Street is said to have been built by one of these Simons, but we do not know which one. The tradition is that the house was already an old one when occupied by Joseph in 1775, so, whichever Simon was the builder, it is almost certain to have been the nesting-place of some of the forebears of the Honorable Calvin Coolidge. There were many other Simons in the other branches of the family, but I feel confident that it must have been one of these other branches that begot the immortal "Simple Simon."

Joseph Coolidge had two sons in their early teens, Joshua, 16, and Joseph, 14, who worked all night with their yoke of oxen building the fortification on Bunker Hill. In the morning they were told that, inasmuch as they had worked all night, they might go home with their oxen and there hold themselves in readiness for a sudden call. They went home, but the battle occurred while they were on their way and they knew nothing about it until it was all over. That is how it came to pass that I am here to tell you this story, for our line descends from the elder brother Joshua.

The old Grove Street house was occupied by my grandfather, John Coolidge, for some twenty years from about 1820 to 1840, when the old gentleman moved to his palatial new house just across the street. The old house was then occupied by my father and I was the last Coolidge born in it in January, 1851.

The only thing concerning this last Coolidge born in the old house is that, although he is a very modest man, he but I want to appeal to you to be loyal to your old stamping-ground and to the bones of your ancestors which rest in yonder cemetery. From the original John Coolidge down, our branch has been born, and lived and died in Watertown. I can find a record of only one man who moved out of town and he subsequently returned and died here.

We cordially welcome you to Watertown and trust you will have a very pleasant time. I am sorry we cannot offer you the cheer that this occasion demands, but the old decanter that used to stand on the sideboard, chiefly for the benefit of the minister, has been placed on the retired list—without a pension.

ST. PATRICK'S PARISH TERCENTENARY YEAR FIELD DAY ON JULY 12

A group of active committees has been busily engaged in making preparations for this year's Tercentenary

ard, John H. Kilfoy, Henry Frissora, Tony Beatrice, Martocchio Brothers, John Welch.

Main Street and Bemis District

Miss Lillian McCafferty, Miss Nellie Courtney, Miss Frances Lyons, Mrs. James Reason, Mrs. Veronica Sandford, Miss Mary Devaney, Miss Elizabeth Shea, Miss Helena McCarthy, Miss Nellie Hoey, Miss Agnes Rooney, Miss Bannister, Miss Frances Barry, Miss Anna Barry, Miss Anna Cahill, Miss Mary Cahill, Miss Catherine Flaherty, Miss Emma Lyons, Miss Helen Lyons, Miss Mary Regan, Miss Nellie Lyons, Miss Owens, Miss Hannah Sullivan, Miss Julia Maguire, Mrs. John Kenney, Mrs. Margaret Kiley, Mrs. Anna Hughes, Mrs. James Sullivan, Mrs. George McCarthy, Mrs. Grace Whyte, Mrs. Lyons, Mrs. Denis Sullivan, Mrs. Gildea, Mrs. Thomas Good, Mrs. Mary O'Neil, Mrs. William Ryan, Mrs. D. Courtney, Mrs. Marie Robillard, William Calnan, Charles Molloy, D. Sullivan, John Ford, James Reason, J. Sullivan, Thomas Tierney, James Sullivan, Jr., Frank O'Reilly, John Kiley, John Leahy, Joseph Leahy.

North Beacon Street District

Miss Mary Morley, Miss Lillian Durkin

Luncheon Served in Tent

Luncheon was served in a large tent on the front lawn, and after luncheon, Mr. William Henry Coolidge, of Manchester, the president of the Coolidge Family Association, opened the business meeting with a welcome to all guests on this most noteworthy occasion. His dry bits of wit made the meeting most enjoyable. Mr. Herbert Coolidge had prepared a most interesting welcome as host, with history of his own family, which he was unable to give, and which was read most pleasingly by his daughter, Miss Delpha Coolidge. The president then introduced a member of each branch of the family, there being descendants of four sons and one daughter of John and Mary Coolidge. Mr. William Coolidge Lane spoke for the youngest branch, Jonathan; Dr. Algernon Coolidge, descendant of this same son, also brought a message; Mr. Joseph Austin Coolidge, of Cambridge, spoke wittily for the second branch, Simon; Dr. Charles Davenport, of Newton, spoke for the descendants of the one daughter, Mary; and Hon. Marcus Coolidge, of Fitchburg, as descendant of the third son, Nathaniel, spoke most amusingly of Will Rogers and democratic Coolidges. All gave much of interest or humor in their brief remarks.

The president called for report of progress as to consideration for a gift or memorial to the Parish of Cottenham, England, where John Coolidge was born, by the chairman, Mrs. Fred Crawford, and the Association voted that the president should appoint a committee to carry forward this excellent enterprise, in honor of their ancestor. The officers who were already serving the Association were unanimously re-elected; namely, Mr. William Henry Coolidge, of Manchester, president; Mr. Francis Lowell Coolidge, of Boston and Milton, vice-president; and Miss Nettie E. Coolidge, of Framingham, secretary-treasurer.

Miss Emma D. Coolidge Speaker

The president then introduced the speaker of the afternoon, a descendant of the eldest son, Ensign John, Miss Emma Downing Coolidge of Newton, historian of the family and chairman of the Genealogical Committee. Miss Coolidge is an author, with many books to her credit, and she has just completed for the Association a Genealogy brought up to date as its share in the celebration of the Tercentenary, a book containing over 350 pages. She is the daughter of John Henry Coolidge, LL.B. of Natick, lawyer and writer, and the grand-daughter of Col. Alexander Coolidge, selectman of Natick, Middlesex County coroner for forty years and commissioned lieutenant of cavalry in 1828 by Governor Levi Lincoln on whose staff he served. Miss Coolidge is a prominent clubwoman in Newton and Massachusetts, and her tercentenary poem, "Our Torch," she read as the closing of her speech.

The "Historical Address" contained many personal bits of history of descendants, as well as accounts of early

Hon. Louis Arthur Coolidge, assistant secretary of the treasury under Pres. Roosevelt, and author of several notable books. Other writers in this branch are Dane Coolidge, author of western stories, of California; Dr. Emelyn Lincoln Coolidge, famous baby specialist, whose articles appear in New York magazines; and Grace Coolidge Pennypacker, author of children's stories.

Many Famous Coolidges

For a descendant of the second son, Simon, Coolidge Corner was named. David Coolidge of Watertown married in 1814 Susan Griggs, of Brookline, and here he had a fine farm near what was later called Coolidge Corner, and two of his descendants had grocery stores at this corner, both of which facts gave the name to the location. A prominent judge, Judge Ashbel Gould Coolidge, of Rutland, Vt., and an educator, Prof. Guy Coolidge, of Wesleyan College, Kentucky, are descended from this son. Three of the most distinguished men of the present day also spring from this son of John and Mary Coolidge; namely, ex-President Calvin Coolidge; Leigh Hill Coolidge, a naval architect of Seattle, Wash., whose models of diesel tugs are world-famous; and Dr. William David Coolidge, of the General Electric Co., Schenectady, N. Y., the greatest physical scientist of the age, who has had bestowed upon him every gold medal that organizations of world science can bestow.

Among descendants of the third son, Nathaniel, owner of the famous fishery weirs, there are three prominent judges: Hon. Frank Wesley Coolidge, of Redfield, S. D.; Judge Henry Hiel Coolidge, and Judge Orville William Coolidge, both of Michigan. There were also many Revolutionary soldiers and World War heroes, among them General Jonathan Coolidge of Waltham. Men prominent in politics, senators, and representatives include Hon. Frederick Spaulding Coolidge, of Westminster, father of Hon. Marcus Coolidge, of Fitchburg, also well-known; Hon. Richard Coolidge, mayor of Medford; and all the Hoars, Senator Samuel; Hon. Ebenezer Rockwood, and Hon. George Frisbee Hoar. One noted family had the architect, David Hill Coolidge; his famous son, Frederick Shurtleff Coolidge, a surgeon; Albert Sprague Coolidge, at whose beautiful Pittsfield home are held annual musical festivals, and donor of the concert hall at the Library of Congress; and the most famous architect in the world today, Charles Allerton Coolidge, of Boston, who designed the Harvard Medical school and dormitories; Leland Stanford, Rockefeller Institute, Chicago Public Library, Art Museum and Law School, besides many beautiful buildings at Boston.

Descendants of the youngest son Jonathan, who was a surveyor and who surveyed the town line between Newton and Watertown, include many well-known diplomats and educators. Prof. Julian Lowell Coolidge, Prof. Archibald Cary Coolidge, and Dr. Algernon Coolidge are known as Har-

(Please Turn to Page 5)

the other was one of the prolonged sessions of the School Committee.

But the real story is this: It was getting well on toward the hour of midnight when there arrived at the 40 and 8 "wreck" a platter of sandwiches and hot coffee, from the Splendid Restaurant.

The man who delivered the edibles said that Dr. Chase, (who happens to be the presiding officer of the School Committee) ordered the repast sent over to the Town Hall. The boys, not to be outdone, passed the sandwiches and coffee to the several candidates who had been initiated into the frills of the 40 and 8. As a matter of fact, the candidates were a little the worse for wear and tear and were in need of something in the way of refreshments.

However, it so happened that the School Committee had ordered the repast for its own membership. When the food was not delivered, Dr. Chase had a second call put in to the "Splendid," and it was not until then that it was learned that the sandwiches had gone to the wrong party. It was too late to retrieve the food, and another order had to be made up for the School Committee which was in session until about "three o'clock in the morning."

SUMMER CAMP SEASON OPENS FOR WATERTOWN CHILDREN

Eighteen Watertown children left town Wednesday morning for the summer camp of the Southern Middlesex Health Association on Lake Massapoag, Sharon. They were in charge of the Board of Health Nurses, and arrived at Sharon before noon. Most of the first day was occupied by registration and assignment of the children to their quarters.

From now until the last of August these children will spend their time playing in the open air on the shore of the lake. This enjoyable summer vacation was made possible by the sale of Christmas seals, by the funds raised at the Health Department whist party, and by the contributions of a number of local organizations.

VETS POSTPONE KIDDIES' DAY TO ARMISTICE CELEBRATION

Burnham-Manning Post 1105, Veterans of Foreign Wars, has voted to postpone its annual Fourth of July Kiddies' program until Armistice Day when it is planned to give the youngsters their annual frolic.

The Post named Commander Frank H. Quinlan and Joseph J. Manning as delegates to the national convention which will be held during August at Baltimore. The alternates are Daniel W. Shedd and Joseph A. Burns.

versal of
ning and
the Watertown
As the
was closely
did the
looked good
defense
which was
C. a few
under their
and his boys
trouble the
all the teams.

Two
and Jim
Sandy
ured the win
W. A. C.
score.
times in the
idan contri
drew a life
triple by
Denucci on a
more runs
when Barnie
lowed by a
Henry Sha
singled but
play when
The W. A. C.
the fourth.
reached first
Lyman and
stunt. Ray P
fect bunt
scoring. Bob
the third base
Singles in the
han and Jim S
more runs for
dy Denucci
fly and Joe
the left field
han pitched
Knights and
by Lefty Mathe
gast toed the rubber

FINAL TRIBUTE TO M

Many friends
death on June
Brooks St., in
Ford (nee) Mary
who passed away
ness with double

Mrs. Ford was
twenty-eight year
marriage in 1922
town where she
friends by her
and charity.

Funeral service
Thursday with a
at the Church
Faneuil, during
was sung by Mr.
which the hymn,
was sung by a
Gordon. Interme
rick's Cemetery,
Rev. J. J. Riley
prayer.

Mrs. Ford is
band, Paul T.,
ton, three small
brother and fath

[illegible] held themselves in readiness for a sudden call. They went home, but the battle occurred while they were on their way and they knew nothing about it until it was all over. That is how it came to pass that I am here to tell you this story, for our line descends from the elder brother Joshua.

The old Grove Street house was occupied by my grandfather, John Coolidge, for some twenty years from about 1820 to 1840, when the old gentleman moved to his palatial new house just across the street. The old house was then occupied by my father and I was the last Coolidge born in it in January, 1851.

The only thing concerning this last Coolidge born in the old house is that, although he is a very modest man, he carries the greatest name of all the Coolidge tribe. He is responsible for the names of two presidents of the United States—Herbert for Hoover and Coolidge for Calvin, but he must have been overlooked as he never secured a position in the Cabinet of either president.

Regrets Tearing Down of Old House

It is to be regretted that this old house was torn down. It might have escaped that fate if the Society for the Preservation of New England Antiquities had been organized earlier, but I am informed that the Watertown Historical Society will erect a recording-stone on the site.

There are interesting traditions of the old fellows who lived there. For instance, my great grandfather, Joshua, was reputed to have hearing as keen as a fox. He had chopping-blocks in the yard of the dwelling. It is said that if he were away over the hill a half a mile distant, he could hear the boys cracking nuts on the chopping blocks, and would utter a mighty roar to the boys to desist because chips of nut-shells might injure the edges of the axes and hatchets.

The farm was a large one and employed a considerable number of men in the summer time, chiefly green Irishmen right over from the bogs of Ireland, or lumbermen from the north of New England. My grandfather's new house had a long ell with three large kitchens. The family kitchen was next to the main house and the second kitchen was for the laboring men. My grandfather, John Coolidge, was a deacon of the Baptist Church. It was his practice always to say grace before meat; also when the men were gathered around the dinner-table it was the old gentleman's custom to carve the meat and see that every man was well served. He would then go forward and dine with the family in the main house. One day, when the men were gathered about the table, he saw the arm of a newly hired lumberman shoot out to the bread-plate. The old gentleman raised his hand, holding the carving knife, and said, "Hold on there, my friend. It is customary here to say a little something before beginning to eat." The man looked up with his mouth open and answered, "All right, Boss, go ahead, say anything you like, you can't turn my stomach."

It was the old man's habit to shave every night before going to bed. He used to draw a chair up to the kitchen-stove which he would use as a table and by the light of a little petticoat whale-oil lamp he would draw enough warm water from the tea-kettle to answer his purpose. One night a green Irishman who knew nobody and had nowhere to go, lounged in the kitchen and took pity on the old man sitting by the stove. He stepped forward, took the lamp in his hand and moved it around grandfather's face as he plied the razor from side to side. When the shaving was finished, the old gentleman said, "Thanks, Pat, but I suppose you noticed I had no mirror."

Joshua Coolidge Remarkable Man

Probably the most distinguished member of our Watertown branch was Joshua Coolidge, a grandson of the Joseph who was killed at the Battle of Lexington and a first cousin of my own father. Joshua was quite a remarkable man. Although a farmer, he acquired by himself a reading knowledge of French and German after he was fifty years of age. He was a great reader, having a large library of his own, and he was one of the founders of the Watertown Free Public Library. He also served in many important town offices. He was an earnest anti-slavery man and a friend of Wendell Phillips. A considerable musician, he played several instruments, and held the position of organist in the Baptist Church in Watertown. He was an intelligent and liberal-minded man. It is said that when the last hymn was sung, prior to the sermon, he would slip out of the church and run over to the neighboring Unitarian church to hear the eminent Rev. John Weiss preach. He would then rush back to play the Doxology for the Baptist church. Among his descendants are a daughter and two granddaughters who are members of this association and who are with us today.

In my youth, Watertown was a beautiful town with neat farms and large estates with velvety lawns. It is now an imperial city of two-tenement dwellings, pleasant time. I am sorry we cannot offer you the cheer that this occasion demands, but the old decanter that used to stand on the sideboard, chiefly for the benefit of the minister, has been placed on the retired list—without a pension.

ST. PATRICK'S PARISH TERCENTENARY YEAR FIELD DAY ON JULY 12

A group of active committees has been busily engaged in making preparations for this year's Tercentenary Field Day of St. Patrick's Parish.

The big event, the finest in the history of the church, will be held on Saltonstall Park on Saturday, July 12th. There will be athletic events for young and old—dashes, potato races, obstacle races, three-legged races. There will be a shot-put competition, broad and high jumps, and everything to make things interesting for all comers.

This year as a special attraction, the Newton Constabulary Band has been engaged, an organization known throughout the state for its proficiency.

There will be four booths, one for each district of the parish. In addition there will be games of skill of all kinds. There has been a series of whist and bridge parties during the past few weeks that have been well attended and enjoyed by all. Each night from now until the Field Day itself there will be a whist and bridge party which it is hoped will be well attended.

The committees which have been working hard and earnestly under the direction of and with the cooperation and support of the pastor, the Rev. Daniel C. Riordan, are as follows:

South Side

Mrs. John Mooney, Mrs. Joseph McElroy, Mrs. Helen Murphy, Miss Katherine Garvin, Miss Helen Healey, Mrs. Joseph Kelley, Mrs. Walter Burke, Mrs. Mary McCarron, Mrs. Mary Morris, Mrs. Garnway, Mrs. Goodman, Miss Margaret Murphy, Mrs. Marion Kelley, Mrs. Garvey, Mrs. Rockett, Miss Madeline Cunniff, Mrs. M. J. McCarthy, Mrs. William Shields, Mrs. Annie Thomas, Mrs. Mary Connors, Mrs. Driscoll, Miss Katherine Cram, Miss Mary Coffey, Mrs. Flanagan, Mrs. Ambrose, Miss Helen Hewitt, Miss Mary Walsh, Mrs. James Kelley, Miss Anna O'Toole, Miss Marion Quinlan, Miss Mary Slamin, Mrs. Munhall, Miss Mary Forbes, John Mooney, William Morris, Thomas Sheridan, Denis Lordan, Louis Perkins, Francis Mooney, Daniel Murphy, Joseph Quinlan, Martin Hynes, Joseph Kelly, Lawrence Connors, Frank Caverley.

North Side Table

Miss Bessie C. Dolan, Miss Anne Norton, Mrs. C. H. Keefe, Mrs. George Farrell, Mrs. Michael Mostowitz, Mrs. George Brackett, Mrs. Thomas Dwyer, Miss Mary Corcoran, Mrs. T. Frederick Grogan, Mrs. Peter A. Leonard, Miss Mary A. Rady, Miss Alice McNally, Miss Margaret Collins, Mrs. Francis Mannix, Mrs. Harriet A. Kelley, Mrs. Julia Paine, Mrs. Louis Depass, Mrs. John Gallagher, Mrs. Augustus Foley, Mrs. James Collins, Mrs. Philip Farley, Mrs. P. Sarsfield Cunniff, Mrs. James Meagher, Mrs. Joseph Moran, Mrs. Charles Mann, Mrs. Joseph Fitzgerald, Miss Alice Dwyer, Mrs. P. H. O'Connell, Mrs. William Sweeney, Miss Margaret Keefe, Miss Annie Stephenson, Miss Mary Sands, Mrs. Frank Broadhurst, Mrs. Harry Houdashell, Mrs. Catherine Wormser, Miss Mary Hyde, Mrs. Alex MacDonald, Miss Anna Hamrock, Mrs. Thomas Nally, Mrs. Anna Roche, Mrs. Thomas Devaney, Miss Ethel Reed, Miss May Doherty, Mrs. Margaret Collins, The Misses McDonnell, Mrs. John Igoe, Miss Frances McMullen, Miss Veronica Hoey, Mrs. Charles Harris, Miss Alice Dardis, Miss Mary Dardis, Miss Elizabeth Leonard, Mrs. Philip Cook, Mrs Annie Regan, Miss Helen Regan, Miss Esther Regan, Miss Mary Miller, Mrs. Fred Miller, Miss Dariah McDonald, Mrs. George Cannon, Mrs. Daniel Sullivan, Mrs. Catherine McAuliffe, Mrs. Lawrence Natoli, Mrs. Charles Hall, James B. Dardis, C. H. Keefe, Dr. T. Frederick Grogan, Michael Harrington, John Hussey, Philip Cook, George Cannon, Lawrence Natoli, Charles Harris, William Hughes, Denis Corbett, Joseph Loughlin, Henry Igoe, Edward Stevens, Robert Stevens, Matthew Carley, Thomas Devaney, Joseph L. Doherty, Edward Doherty, Arthur Perkins, Patrick Callahan, John Igoe, Peter A. Leon[illegible] Anna Cahill, Miss Mary Cahill, Miss Catherine Flaherty, Miss Emma Lyons, Miss Helen Lyons, Miss Mary Regan, Miss Nellie Lyons, Miss Owens, Miss Hannah Sullivan, Miss Julia Maguire, Mrs. John Kenney, Mrs. Margaret Kiley, Mrs. Anna Hughes, Mrs. James Sullivan, Mrs. George McCarthy, Mrs. Grace Whyte, Mrs. Lyons, Mrs. Denis Sullivan, Mrs. Gildea, Mrs. Thomas Good, Mrs. Mary O'Neil, Mrs. William Ryan, Mrs. D. Courtney, Mrs. Marie Robillard, William Calnan, Charles Molloy, D. Sullivan, John Ford, James Reason, J. Sullivan, Thomas Tierney, James Sullivan, Jr., Frank O'Reilly, John Kiley, John Leahy, Joseph Leahy.

North Beacon Street District

Miss Mary Morley, Miss Lillian Durkin, Mrs. John McAteer, Mrs. Jennie Gavin, Mrs. John J. Mulhern, Mrs. Thomas Hanley, Mrs. John Gallagher, Mrs. James Carroll, Mrs. Patrick Ryan, Mrs. Michael Cotter, Mrs. Felix Rando, Mrs. John Cunniff, Mrs. Stephen Moynihan, Mrs. Albert Comstock, Mrs. James Russell, Mrs. Edward Morley, Mrs. Sadie Nichols, Mrs. Delia Durkin, Mrs. Lena Dooley, Mrs. Patrick Higgins, Mrs. John Ford, Mrs. Mary Finnegan, Miss Mary Colligan, Miss Mary Carroll, Miss Mary Hanley, Miss Anna Twohig, Miss Rose McNeil, Miss Elizabeth Ford, Miss Cecilia Ford, Miss Mary Conway, Miss Catherine Waldron, Miss Sheila Moynihan, Miss Mary Carroll, Miss Agnes Farraher.

NEW AUXILIARY MEMBER DAUGHTER OF VETERAN

Watertown Legion Auxiliary Unit has a new member, the sixteen year old daughter of Adjutant and Mrs. Ellery Dodge.

The new member, Margaret Dodge, is the only daughter of a World War veteran enrolled in the Auxiliary Unit who has attained the age which permits her to become a member with full voting privileges.

Miss Dodge, a High School student, who is possessed of considerable artistic ability, having done some exceptional poster work for the Auxiliary and other organizations, was given a warm welcome at the meeting of the Unit Monday evening. Like her father, Adjutant Ellery Dodge of the Legion Post, she is an untiring worker.

MALONEY—CORCORAN

At the Sacred Heart Church on Monday evening, June 30, Miss Helen Cecelia Corcoran was united in marriage to Mr. William Edward Maloney. The double ring ceremony was performed by the Rev. Edward J. Sullivan.

The bride was gowned in yellow chiffon, with yellow horsehair hat to match, and carried a bouquet of yellow roses. Attending the bridal couple were Miss Laura E. Monahan of Watertown and James J. Lyons of Newton. Miss Monahan was prettily dressed in nile green chiffon with black horsehair hat, and carried a bouquet of butterfly roses.

After the ceremony a reception was held at the Hotel Buckminster, Boston, for the bridal party and immediate relatives only.

The bride and groom have been residents of Watertown since childhood, both having attended St. Patrick's grammar and high schools; they are graduates in the class of 1919. The bridesmaid is also a Watertown girl and a member of the same class. She has been a close friend of the bride for many years.

The groom is also known in Watertown by many of his friends as having a pleasing tenor voice, and has sung on several occasions at Watertown fetes.

After a trip over the road to New Hampshire's mountains, the bride and groom will be at home to their friends at 16 St. Mary's St., Watertown.

NOTES

FURTHER GENEALOGY...

As mentioned in the Introduction, included in the inherited artifacts was a book written by Emma Downing Coolidge, entitled *Descendants of John and Mary Coolidge of Watertown, Massachusetts 1630*. John and Mary Coolidge traveled from England to America in 1630 during the second wave of those first American Colonists. President J. Calvin Coolidge was a descendant of John and Mary's second son; my family descends from their eldest son—"Ensign" John Coolidge.

Ensign John Coolidge served in King Philip's War and saved many families from massacre by applying his carpentry skills. (An "Ensign" was equal to that of a second lieutenant.) On October 25, 1675, Ensign John and his 14-year-old son, also named John, traveled to Brookfield, Massachusetts, and built lodgings and blockades to help protect the soldiers from the Indians. 14-year-old John (Jr.) is recorded as the youngest soldier to serve in King Philip's War.

John (Jr.) Coolidge (born in 1661/2) had nine children. The first was named Isaac, born in 1685. Major Isaac Coolidge had six children; the second was named John and was born on June 21, 1714. Captain John Coolidge was deputy sheriff under King George III. Captain John Coolidge had 11 children, the fourth of which was Isaac, born on Aug. 29, 1747. Isaac Coolidge had nine children, the third of which was Asa, born on May 21, 1774. Asa Coolidge moved to Orange, Massachusetts, in May of 1810 and had eleven children; the eighth was Napoleon B. Coolidge, born June 18, 1809. Napoleon resided in Orange/New Salem and had seven children; the fourth was Benjamin Franklin Coolidge, born October 19, 1841. He and his wife, Dorothy Adeline Jones, had a son named Harry Lyman Coolidge, born in New Salem, Massachusetts, on December 14, 1870.

Harry Lyman Coolidge married Lillie B. Pierce. They had two children—my grandfather, Franklin Pierce Coolidge, born on October 9, 1898, in Athol, Massachusetts, and my Aunt Ellen. Franklin married Doris Elizabeth Nesbit, who was born on August 29, 1907, in Westfield, Massachusetts. Franklin and Doris had two children—my uncle, John Calvin Coolidge, born on April 24, 1926, and my mother, Ann Nesbit Coolidge, born on February 18, 1929.

ABOUT CLIMBING ANGEL PUBLISHING

Climbing Angel Publishing exists for the purpose of sharing stories of hope and encouragement, aiding in the gathering together of community, and supporting the process of betterment. The following books are available at ClimbingAngel.com and major bookstores.

ADULT BOOKS: (Romans 8:28-30)

In His Image, by Sam Polson (English, Romanian, & Mandarin)
By Faith, by Sam Polson (English & Romanian)
My Birthday Gift to Jesus, by Lisa Soland
Without Ceasing, by Dr. Dennis Davidson
SonLight: Daily Light from the Pages of God's Word, by Sam Polson
Corona Victus: Conquering the Virus of Fear, by Sam Polson
Art Bushing: His Diary, Letters, & Photographs of WWII, by Art Bushing
Art & Dotty: His Diary, Their Letters & Photographs of WWII, by Art Bushing
Trimisul, by Stan Johnson (Romanian)
Life Changing Prayer, by Sam Polson
The Climbing Angel Christmas Treasury, by a variety of authors
J. Calvin Coolidge: Letters from the Korean War

CHILDREN'S BOOKS: (Philippians 4:8)

The Christmas Tree Angel, by Lisa Soland
The Unmade Moose, by Lisa Soland
Thump, by Lisa Soland
Somebunny To Love, by Lisa Soland (English & Mandarin)
The Truth About God's Rainbow, by Lisa Soland
God's Promises, by Lisa Soland
The Boy & The Bagel Necklace, by Lisa Soland
God's Hands and Feet, by Lisa Soland
I Like To Be Quiet, by Joni Caldwell
Wheels Off!, by Karlie Saumier
Ella's Trip of a Lifetime, by Melanie Ewbank
Because You Are Mine, by Gayle Childress Greene
Jeremy Plays the Blues, by Amy Oden Simpson
Bad Hair Day, by Jasmyne Simpkins
I Like To Read, by Joni Caldwell
Trunks Up!, by Karlie Saumier
Perusha's Paradise, by Bette Reed Smith
Ruby and the Treasure Within, by Tonya Celeste Hobbs

www.ingramcontent.com/pod-product-compliance
Lightning Source LLC
Chambersburg PA
CBHW031007190726
48286CB00003BA/721

* 9 7 8 1 9 5 6 2 1 8 1 9 0 *